Ancient Egyptian Religion

KING SETI I AND THE GODDESS ISIS, ABYDOS

Ancient Egyptian Religion

An Interpretation

by H. FRANKFORT

Research Professor of Oriental Archaeology
in the University of Chicago

HARPER TORCHBOOKS ❧ The Cloister Library

HARPER & ROW, PUBLISHERS

New York

Preface

EGYPTIAN religion aroused the interest of the West long before the hieroglyphs were deciphered. The fabulous antiquity of Egyptian civilization and its stupendous ruins have always suggested a background of profound wisdom. Plutarch set the fashion of writing under that impression, and it has continued to the present day. But the decipherment of the documents has disappointed centuries of expectation: it revealed a remarkable lack of philosophical content, at least in a form which we can assimilate. Instead the texts introduce us to an apparent jungle of religious matter, so impenetrable to our understanding that Egyptologists have increasingly shunned the task of interpretation.

Erman, the first to base a description of Egyptian religion on a full understanding of the language, gave in 1905 a masterly but patronizing account of weird myths, doctrines, and usages, while the peculiarly religious values which these contained remained hidden from his lucid rationalism.[1] Breasted succeeded in taking Egyptian religion seriously, but only at the cost of its integrity; he described in 1912 a "Development of Religion and Thought in Ancient Egypt" towards ethical ideals which pertain to biblical but not to ancient Egyptian religion.[2] Since then interpretation has

---

[1] Adolf Erman, *Die Religion der alten Aegypter, ihr Werden und Vergehen in vier Jahrtausenden* (Berlin, 1934). The original edition was translated by A. S. Griffith: *A Handbook of Egyptian Religion* (London, 1907).
[2] James Henry Breasted, *Development of Religion and Thought in Ancient Egypt* (New York, 1912). This book, a pioneer work at the time of its

lagged. W. B. Kristensen in Leiden continued the elucida-
tion of specific symbols, but the most prolific writers—Kees
and his followers—assumed towards our subject a scien-
tist's rather than a scholar's attitude: while ostensibly concerned with religion, they were really absorbed in the task
of bringing order to a confused mass of material.

Men of this school have dominated the subject for the
last twenty or thirty years; [3] they possess a splendid knowledge of the texts and have enriched our information greatly.
But in reading their books you would never think that the
gods they discuss once moved men to acts of worship. Moreover, they deny—explicitly or by implication—that one can
speak of Egyptian religion as such. They see a number of
unrelated local cults which existed side by side; and they
even succeed in explaining the fact that certain beliefs were
held by *all* Egyptians without referring to religion at all.
According to their view (and it is widely accepted today)
the nation-wide validity of a doctrine was always the consequence of *political* power, exercised at one time or another by the city of its origin. These men, therefore, evade
the problem altogether; for when we ask how people in
the vanguard of civilization could believe what their documents proclaim, it is not relevant to answer that the Amon
priests at Thebes induced a king of Theban origin to propa-
gate the cult of Amon.

publication, is still valuable. In Breasted's later treatment of the same subject, *The Dawn of Conscience* (New York, 1934), the evolutionary bias
characteristic of his generation carried him away, but this tendency was
checked in the earlier work by the close contact with the actual texts which
he maintained throughout.

[3] Jacques Vandier, *La religion égyptienne,* " 'Mana'; introduction à l'histoire des religions" (Paris, 1944) is the best up-to-date handbook of Egyptian religion. It gives a full account of the present state of our knowledge
and of the prevalent theories, and although Vandier does not reject these,
he does indicate in several places their inherent improbability or their
hypothetical character.

Scholars who deal with our subject in this manner not only ignore religion as a phenomenon *sui generis,* but are unable to see the wood for the trees. The unity of the Egyptian people is an established fact with respect to language, material culture, and even physique. It would be absurd to assume that there did not exist a corresponding unity in the domain of the spirit. We shall, in fact, attempt to discover that unity in the course of this book. We shall go beyond the local and temporal differences in cults and dogmas, and look for those trends and qualities that seem to have shaped the character of Egyptian religion as a whole. This means, of course, that we shall have to disregard a great many details, however interesting they may be. We shall have to concentrate on what appear to have been the main religious preoccupations—sometimes the religious obsessions—of a highly civilized people. And we shall find that it is possible to view the monstrous as well as the profound in Egyptian religion—with amazement perhaps, but also with respect.

It will appear, moreover, that the Egyptian doctrines are not without coherence. They were rooted in a single basic conviction, to wit that the universe is essentially static. The Egyptian held that he lived in a changeless world. It is irrelevant that his view, whether it be applied to nature or to society, seems untenable to us. What matters is that the Egyptian held it, and that it informed not only his theology but also his moral and political philosophy. Not as an articulate doctrine, but nevertheless decisively, it determined the forms he gave to his state and his society, to his literature and his art. In fact, we have recognized the Egyptian's view of the world only through the study of those forms, and we are summarizing in this Preface, not an *a priori*

opinion, but the conclusion reached in the course of work
which extended over a number of years. In this book we
have, as it were, approached the Egyptians' beliefs from five
distinct directions and found each time that these beliefs
possessed a clearly recognizable individuality. The peculiar character of Egyptian religion appeared to derive precisely from an implicit assumption that only the changeless
is ultimately significant.

It is true, of course, that Egyptian beliefs were in themselves subject to change; but we have not discussed those
which were peculiar to a limited period. It may one day be
possible to write a history of Egyptian religion describing
the changes which it underwent in the course of time. At
present we are still endeavoring to recognize what was the
subject of those changes. Before tracing the history we
should establish the identity of Egyptian religion.

It may be argued that such an attempt is, even now, pre-
mature: many texts are still unpublished, others are only
preserved in fragments, others again are obscure. But we
have gradually come to reject this view as defeatist. During
many years of constant preoccupation with religious phenomena of the Ancient Near East we have become increasingly convinced that the material allows us to define at least
some essentials of Egyptian beliefs. Moreover, the textual
difficulties are not the main obstacle to our understanding
—if they were, it would be presumptuous for an archaeolo-
gist to deal with the subject at all. Those difficulties are ag-
gravated by the limitations which a nineteenth-century
viewpoint—whether evolutionary or rationalistic—imposed upon scholars who were the otherwise undisputed
masters of Egyptology. We have discussed this matter at
the beginning of this Preface; the attitudes described there

agree in obscuring the profound difference in mentality
which separates the ancients from ourselves. Yet an awareness of that difference is a prerequisite of true understanding, and in two recent publications an attempt has been
made to define its scope. The opening and concluding chapters of *The Intellectual Adventure of Ancient Man* (Chicago, 1946) describe the distinction between the mythopoeic thought of the ancients and the critical thought of
modern times. In *Kingship and the Gods* (Chicago, 1948)
we have attempted to collect and to interpret all the evidence bearing on one single subject, the integration of society and nature mediated by the king.

The present work proceeds on the assumption that these
earlier publications have justified our method by demon-
strating that ancient thought can be comprehended once
its own peculiar coherence is discovered. We have therefore, in this book, reduced critical remarks to a minimum.
But one general acknowledgement must be made here.
This work was written while Mrs. H. A. Groenewegen-
Frankfort was engaged upon her book, *Space and Time in
the Representational Art of the Ancient Near East*. Many
problems were a matter of concern to both of us, and I have
profited from our discussions in more ways than I can
specify.

The chapters which follow are enlarged versions of lectures sponsored by the American Council of Learned So-
cieties.[4] The illustrations—both textual and pictorial—are
fewer than I could have wished, and my statements may

---

[4] These were delivered at Chicago, Columbia, Indiana, Oregon, and Yale
universities; at Beloit, Bryn Mawr, Dropsie, Haverford, Oberlin, and
Swarthmore colleges; at the Garrett Biblical Institute, Evanston; at the
Boston Museum of Fine Arts, the Semitic Museum at Harvard, and the
University Museum at Philadelphia.

consequently appear a little apodictic. But figures and quotations were selected as representative examples of a large body of evidence which could not be discussed in full without changing the scope and purpose of the work. The references to published translations of the texts should enable the non-specialist reader to enlarge his knowledge of the relevant material.

The crested ibis, which appears on the cover and title page, is a hieroglyph rendering the word *akh*. The reader of chapters 3 and 4 will realize why it was thought an appropriate ornament for our interpretation of ancient Egyptian religion.

H. FRANKFORT

The Oriental Institute, Chicago
Kimmeridge, near Corfe Castle, Dorset

Contents

5. Change and Permanence in Literature and Art

Illustrations

Chronological Table

Approximate date B.C.	Period	Kings mentioned
5000(?)–3100	Predynastic period	
3100	Unification of the country and founding of a dual monarchy	Narmer ("Menes")
3100–2600	Dynasties I–III	Djoser
2600–2180	Old Kingdom (Dynasties IV–VI)	Khufu (Cheops) Khafre Menkaure Sahure Pepi II
2180–2000	First Intermediate period	Merikare Mentuhotep
2000–1780	Middle Kingdom (Dynasties XII–XIII)	Amenemhet I Senusert I Senusert III Amenemhet III
1780–1580	Second Intermediate period (Hyksos invasion)	
1580–1085	New Kingdom (Dynasties XVIII–XX)	Hatshepsut Tuthmosis III Amenhotep III Akhenaten Tutankhamen Haremhab Seti I Ramses II Ramses III

Ancient Egyptian Religion

1

The Egyptian Gods

THE GODS AND THEIR SYMBOLS

RELIGION as we Westerners know it derives its character
and its unity from two circumstances: it centers on the
revelation of a single god, and it contains a message
which must be transmitted. The Torah, the Gospels, and
Islam contain teachings sufficiently coherent for exposi-
tion. The Gospel and Islam must, moreover, be preached
to the unconverted. In the whole of the ancient world
there is only one religion with similar characteristics: the
monotheistic cult of the sun introduced by the heretic
Pharaoh Akhenaten. And Akhenaten was a heretic precisely in this: that he denied recognition to all but one god
and attempted to convert those who thought otherwise.
His attitude presents no problem to us; we acknowledge
a conviction too deep for tolerance. But Egyptian religion was not exclusive. It recognized an unlimited number
of gods. It possessed neither a central dogma nor a holy
book. It could flourish without postulating one basic truth.

We find, then, in Egyptian religion a number of doctrines which strike us as contradictory; but it is sheer presumption to accuse the ancients of muddleheadedness on
this score. In a recent book the reason and the meaning of
this apparent confusion have been explained.[1] I can only

[1] *The Intellectual Adventure of Ancient Man* (Chicago, University of Chicago Press, 1946).

summarize the argument here in a few sentences. The ancients did not attempt to solve the ultimate problems confronting man by a single and coherent theory; that has been the method of approach since the time of the Greeks. Ancient thought—mythopoeic, "myth-making" thought— admitted side by side certain *limited* insights, which were held to be *simultaneously* valid, each in its own proper context, each corresponding to a definite avenue of approach. I have called this "multiplicity of approaches," and we shall find many examples of it as we proceed. At the moment I want to point out that this habit of thought agrees with the basic experience of polytheism.

Polytheism is sustained by man's experience of a universe alive from end to end. Powers confront man wherever he moves, and in the immediacy of these confrontations the question of their ultimate unity does not arise. There are many gods—one cannot know how many; a small handbook of Egyptian religion enumerates more than eighty. How, then, are they recognized? Here we may well use the evidence collected by anthropologists among living believers in polytheism. It appears that superhuman powers reveal themselves sometimes in a curiously accidental manner. For instance, a West African native is on an important expedition when he suddenly stumbles over a stone. He cries out: "Ha! Are you there?" —and takes the stone with him. The stone had, as it were, given a hint that it was powerful, and the Negro strengthened himself by taking possession of it.[2] Under normal conditions he might not have taken notice of the obstacle that tripped him up, but the importance of the

[2] After G. Van der Leeuw, *Religion in Essence and Manifestation*, tr. J. E. Turner (New York, 1938), p. 37.

expedition had created the emotional tension which makes man receptive to signs of a supernatural order.[3] Note that at the very moment that the stone reveals its immanent power, it acquires the quality of a person, for the native exclaims: "Are you there?" The next thing to observe is that such impact on a power in the outside world may be experienced as either of fleeting or of lasting significance. It will be of permanent significance especially when the community accepts it as valid and a cult is consequently established. For instance, an Ewe Negro enters the bush and finds there a piece of iron. Returning home he falls ill, and the priests explain that a divinity is manifesting its potency in the iron and that henceforth the village should worship it.[4]

It seems to me that these examples throw some light upon the fact that Egypt knew a large number of gods and an astonishing variety of cult-objects. But our examples do not answer the question *why* certain experiences acquired a lasting significance (the iron) while others (the stone) did not. They show that we need not expect to be able to answer this question in relation to Egyptian cults, and we should do well to retain from our excursion among modern savages a certain skepticism as to the value of symbols and sacred objects as indicators of the meaning which the gods designated may have had for their worshipers. If many of the sacred objects seem devoid of mystery or meaning to us, it may well be that they were originally connected with the cult in a loose and accidental manner, mere adjuncts to an emotional reality from which the cult continued to draw its life but which we can neither recapture nor reconstruct. On the

[3] See below, end of Chapter 2.   [4] After Van der Leeuw.

other hand, certain sacred objects possessed a deeper, a truly symbolical significance, and in such a case the relation between the deity and the object is capable of being understood. This is so, for instance, when the name of the goddess Isis is written as if it simply meant "throne," while she is also depicted with the throne as her distinctive attribute (Figure 1).

We know that many peoples consider the insignia of royalty to be charged with the superhuman power of kingship. Among these objects the throne occupies a special place: the prince who seats himself upon it at the coronation arises king. The throne "makes" the king—the term occurs in Egyptian texts—and so the throne, Isis, is the "mother" of the king. This expression might be viewed as a metaphor, but the evidence shows that it was not (Frontispiece). The bond between the king and the throne was the intimate one between his person and the power which made him king. Now a power was not recognized objectively, as the result of an intellectual effort on the part of man. We have seen that the power reveals itself; it is recognized in the relationship of "I and thou"; it has the quality of a person.[5] The throne which "made" the king is comprehended as a mother, and thus it may be the object of profound and complex feelings. If we should try to resolve the complexity, we should merely be falsifying the evidence. We can neither say that Isis was originally the throne personified, nor that the throne acquired a transcendental quality because it was conceived as a mother. The two notions are fundamentally correlated, and mythopoeic thought expresses such a bond as identity. The throne made manifest a divine power which

[5] *The Intellectual Adventure of Ancient Man,* Ch. I.

changed one of several princes into a king fit to rule. The awe felt before this manifestation of power became articulate in the adoration of the mother-goddess. There is no question of any evolution from a simpler to a complex notion. Complexity is of the essence of the relationship between man and deity. As early as the First Dynasty a Pharaoh calls himself "son of Isis." [6] We do observe a historical development, but that concerns not the goddess but her cult. Originally Isis was significant only in her relation to the king; subsequently—and especially through the myth of Osiris, which we shall discuss later—she brought consolation to all men, and three thousand years after the first appearance of her name in Egypt, monuments were being erected to her throughout the Roman Empire, up to its very borders on the Rhine and the Danube.

Our discussion of Isis illustrates one possible relationship between the gods and their symbols. Another possibility, as we have said already, is that the symbol lacks all deeper significance. This thought is especially disturbing because the symbols loom very large in our sources; in fact, they constitute in the case of many a god all— or almost all—we know about him. Moreover, since symbols are definite and distinct, they offer a delusive hold to modern research. And so one talks glibly of fetishes, sungods, ram-gods, falcon-gods, and so forth—as if the precision of those terms had any reference to the gods themselves! We must not generalize in this manner. Sometimes the symbol tells us something about a god, sometimes it does not; and mostly the evidence on hand does not allow

[6] W. M. Flinders Petrie, *The Royal Tombs of the First Dynasty* (London, 1901), II, Pl. II, Nos. 13, 14.

us to decide one way or the other. But in any case the use of classificatory or generic terms in connection with the gods bars the road to understanding; for this can only be reached, if at all, by a circumspect interpretation of each individual case.

SACRED ANIMALS AND OTHERNESS

There is one generic term which is most difficult to avoid when we discuss Egyptian religion. That is the word "animal-gods." It should not be used, as we shall show in a moment. But we must admit—and the Greek, Roman, and early Christian writers too were struck by the fact —that animals play an altogether unusual role in Egyptian religion. We cannot evade the issue by referring back to what we said a moment ago, namely, that the origin of cults is beyond our ken and that we shall never know how certain gods came to be associated with certain animals. There are too many gods showing such an association and their cult is too widespread for us to pretend to understand Egyptian religion without at least a tentative explanation of this its most baffling, most persistent, and to us most alien feature.

It is wrong to say that the worship of animals is a survival from a primitive stratum of Egyptian religion. This view is often encountered and is supported by some plausible arguments. It is said that these cults are often of purely local significance; that they sometimes center on quite insignificant creatures like the centipede or the toad (Figure 6); and that we must therefore place the sacred animals on a par with certain sacred objects, like the crossed arrows of the goddess Neith, and consider all these symbols as mere emblems of—and means of promoting—tribal unity. Some scholars have even interpreted them as totems. But the characteristic features of totemism, such as the claim of descent from the totem, its sacrifice for a ceremonial feast of the clan, and exogamy, can not be found in Egyptian sources.[7] Moreover, any treatment of the sacred animals which stresses their local or political significance at the expense of their religious importance flies in the face of the evidence. It is undeniable that there is something altogether peculiar about the meaning which animals possessed for the Egyptians. Elsewhere, in Africa or North America, for example, it seems that either the terror of animal strength, or the strong bond, the mutual dependence of man and beast (in the case of cattle cults, for instance), explains animal worship. But in Egypt *the animal as such,* irrespective of its specific nature, seems to possess religious significance; and the significance was so great that even the mature speculation of later times rarely dispensed with animal forms in plastic or literary images referring to the gods.

But there was nothing metaphorical in the connection between god and animal in Egypt. It is not as if certain divine qualities were made articulate by the creature, in the way the eagle elucidates the character of Zeus. We observe, on the contrary, a strange link between divinity and actual beast, so that in times of decadence animal worship may gain a horrible concreteness. Then one finds mummified cats, dogs, falcons, bulls, crocodiles, and so forth, buried by the hundreds in vast cemeteries which fill the Egyptologist with painful embarrassment—for this,

[7] A. van Gennep, *L'Etat actuel du problème totémique* (Paris, 1922).

we must admit, is polytheism with a vengeance. Nevertheless, these are grotesque but significant symptoms of a characteristic trait in Egyptian religion.

To understand this trait, we should first realize that the relation between a god and his animal may vary greatly. If Horus is said to be a falcon whose eyes are sun and moon and whose breath is the cooling north wind, we may think that this was a mere image to describe an impressive god of the sky. But the god was depicted as a bird from the earliest times and was apparently believed to be manifest either in individual birds or in the species (Figure 7). Thoth was manifest in the moon, but also in the baboon (Figure 3) and in the ibis (Figure 4), and we do not know whether any relations were thought to exist between these different symbols, and if so, what they were.[8] The relation between the Mnevis bull and the sun-god Re, and between the Apis bull and the earth-god Ptah, was different again. Ptah was never depicted as a bull or believed to be incarnate in a bull; but the Apis bull was called "The living Apis, the herald of Ptah, who carries the truth upwards to him of the lovely face (Ptah)." The Mnevis bull bore a similar title in connection with Re. We have to deal here, moreover, not with a species considered sacred, but with one individual identified by certain marks, not as the incarnation, but as the divine servant of the god. Other deities were regularly imagined in animal shapes but even in their case the incarnation did not limit—it did not even define—their powers. Anubis, for instance,

[8] In Fig. 3 the baboon carries the moon symbol on his head; in Fig. 4 the ibis is confronted by two small baboons flanking the goddess Maat. Thoth as scribe of the gods is closely associated with this personification of divine order, truth, justice (pp. 53 ff.). Thoth and Maat also appear together in the sun boat, which follows an unalterably "right" course. It is the association of moon, baboon, and ibis which remains obscure.

was most commonly shown as a reclining jackal but he was by no means a deified animal. Already in the earliest texts in which he is mentioned, he appears as the god of the desert cemeteries. He ensured proper burial and when mummification became common he counted as the master of embalmment. The god was depicted in papyri and reliefs with a human body and a jackal's head (Figure 2).

Such hybrid forms are common in Egyptian art and the usual evolutionary theory explains them as "transitional forms," intermediate between the "crude" cult of animals and the anthropomorphic gods of a more enlightened age. This theory ignores the fact that the earliest divine statues which have been preserved represent the god Min in human shape.[9] Conversely, we find to the very end of Egypt's independence that gods were believed to be manifest in animals. The goddess Hathor appears, for instance, in late papyri and even in royal statues as a cow (Figure 12). Yet she was rendered already in the First Dynasty, on the Palette of Narmer, with a human face, cow's horns, and cow's ears. This early appearance of human features was to be expected, for a god is personified power, and personification need not, but easily may, call up the human image. In any case, the gods were not confined to a single mode of manifestation. We have seen that Thoth appeared as moon, baboon, and ibis. He was also depicted as an ibis-headed man (Figure 5). To speak here of a transitional form seems pointless. There was no need for a transition. The god appeared as he desired, in one of his known manifestations. On the other hand, there was a definite need to distinguish deities when they were depicted in human shape, and in such an array the ibis-headed figure identified Thoth. I suspect that the Egyptians did not intend their hybrid designs as renderings of an imagined reality at all and that we should not take the animal-headed gods at their face value. These designs were probably pictograms, not portraits. Hathor, usually depicted as a cow (Figures 12, 25), a woman's face with cow's ears (Figure 11), or as a woman wearing a crown of cow's horns (like Isis in the Frontispiece), appears very rarely as a cow-headed woman (Figure 14); the meaning would be: This is the goddess who is manifest in the cow.[10] The animal-headed figures are quite unorganic and mechanical; it makes no difference whether a quadruped's head (Figures 2, 14), an ibis' neck (Figure 5), or a snake's forepart emerge from the human shoulder. That again would be easily explained if they were only ideograms, and this interpretation is corroborated by the truly vital character of the few monsters invented by the Egyptians: Taurt (Figure 13), for instance, is convincing even though she is composed of incongruous parts: the head of a hippopotamus, the back and tail of a crocodile, the breasts of a woman, and the claws of a lion.

Our rapid survey of the various relationships between gods and animals in Egypt does not clarify the role of the latter. But the very absence of a general rule and the variety of the creatures involved suggests, it seems to me, that what in these relationships became articulate was an underlying religious awe felt before all animal life; in other words, it would seem that *animals as such* pos-

---

[10] Occasionally the graphic representations influence the texts in their turn so that they read as if the animal-headed form did exist. The same is true of the human-headed Ba-bird; see p. 97 below.

sessed religious significance for the Egyptians. Their attitude might well have arisen from a religious interpretation of the animals' *otherness*. A recognition of *otherness* is implied in all specifically religious feeling, as Otto [11] has shown. We assume, then, that the Egyptian interpreted the nonhuman as superhuman, in particular when he saw it in animals—in their inarticulate wisdom, their certainty, their unhesitating achievement, and above all in their static reality. With animals the continual succession of generations brought no change; and this is not an abstract and far-fetched argument but something which suggested itself also to Keats for instance; in the "Ode to a Nightingale" he writes:

> Thou wast not born for death, immortal Bird!
> No hungry generations tread thee down;
> The voice I hear this passing night was heard
> In ancient days by emperor and clown . . .

The animals never change, and in this respect especially they would appear to share—in a degree unknown to man —the fundamental nature of creation. We shall see in the following chapters that the Egyptians viewed their living universe as a rhythmic movement contained within an unchanging whole. Even their social order reflected this view; in fact, it determined their outlook to such an extent that it can only be understood as an intuitive—and therefore binding—interpretation of the world order. Now humanity would not appear to exist in this manner; in human beings individual characteristics outbalance generic resemblances. But the animals exist in their unchanging species, following their predestined modes of life, irre-

[11] Rudolf Otto, *The Idea of the Holy* (Oxford, 1943).

spective of the replacement of individuals. Thus animal life would appear superhuman to the Egyptian in that it shared directly, patently, in the static life of the universe. For that reason recognition of the animals' *otherness* would be, for the Egyptian, recognition of the divine.

This interpretation of the animal cults of Egypt requires qualification in two respects; it depends, of course, on the strength which the vision of an unchanging universe can be proved to have possessed in Egypt, and it requires therefore the cumulative evidence of the subsequent chapters. And, furthermore, even if it is true that animals in general were capable of inspiring all Egyptians with a feeling of religious awe, that feeling assumed definite and different forms in each of the ensuing cults. Their variety is reflected in the relationships which were claimed to exist between gods and animals, whether individuals or whole species. The working out of such details falls outside the scope of this book. We shall merely say that some were worshiped in a very restricted area only, while others found recognition throughout the country.

COSMIC GODS AND HUMAN PROBLEMS

Some of the animals were even associated with the great cosmic gods. Sun and earth; sky and air; and water, as the element from which all life arose—these were gods which all Egyptians recognized. It has been said that the worship of such gods is too "advanced" to be assumed for early times, but this theory is not only at variance with anthropological evidence, but with simple reason: If the gods are powers who reveal themselves, it would surely be absurd to assume that the great powers in nature would not have been recognized as gods by all Egyptians from the begin-

ning. We should expect these gods to differ greatly from
those to whom we have referred so far. The difference
exists but is elusive. The most obvious distinction, namely,
that the cosmic gods are depicted in human shape, is not
a fundamental one. On the one hand, a deity such as
Hathor, who is manifest in a cow, is also depicted in human shape. On the other hand, Nut, the sky, is depicted
as a woman, but also, in her aspect as mother of sun and
stars, as a cow; [12] the sun may be rendered as a falcon
or a falcon-headed man wearing the sun disk as a crown.
In fact, the generic term "cosmic gods" is hardly less misleading than any other generalization, for the toad Heqt,
who assisted women in childbirth (Figure 6), was as much
a power in nature as the moon. The difference which exists
lies, however, in the power of appeal of those great gods
whom we have called cosmic gods. They were centers
around which speculative thought crystallized. The mystery of animal life must needs remain ineffable. But cosmic
phenomena such as the course of sun or moon, or the
changeless rhythm of the seasons, reveal not only transcendent power but also order. In this lies their relevancy
to the affairs of man. They enable man to find, intuitively
and imaginatively, answers to problems of his own existence: the problem of justice as the order of human society,
the problem of survival after death as the desired order
of human life, or even the problem of meaning as related
to the order of existence. I do not mean to suggest that
the mere observation of the sun, for instance, raised the
problem of spontaneous creation or of rebirth after death;
but it would be equally incorrect, I think, to assume that

[12] On the cow as symbol of motherhood, and on the religious significance
of cattle images in Egypt, see my *Kingship and the Gods,* Ch. 14.

such problems were articulate in man's mind before he
projected them in the sky. When the sun was an object,
not of observation but of contemplation, the problems we
mentioned became articulate in the conception of the cosmic god; and the attributes of the god—as distinct from the
natural phenomenon—implied the recognition of such
problems. There is here, then, correlation in the strictest
sense of the word, a correlation such as we once before
observed in discussing Isis and the throne. But in the case
of the cosmic gods the number of possible correlations
presents a complication: While the natural phenomena are
distinct and irreducible, several among them may be significant for one and the same problem; for instance, the
problem of life and death is correlated with the sun's daily
rising, but also with the circumpolar stars which never
set, and, yet again, with the annual sprouting of the grain.
Conversely, one single natural phenomenon may be significant for several distinct problems: for example, the
sun's life-giving power makes him appear as the creator,
the source of all existence; but his daily rising indicates a
victory over the darkness of death, and his unalterable
course through the sky exemplifies justice.

Abstractly formulated in this manner, the coexistence
of different correlations of problems and phenomena presents no difficulties. It is in the concrete imagery of the
Egyptian texts and designs that they become disturbing to
us; here lies the main source of the inconsistencies which
have baffled and exasperated modern students of Egyptian
religion. Let us first consider the inconsistencies which
appear when a single cosmic power, the sun, is correlated
with several problems. The sun-god, Re, is made to say in
one text where he speaks as the creator:

Only after I came into being did all that was created come into being.[13]

Similarly a morning-hymn addresses the sun as follows:

Divine youth who came into being out of thyself.[14]

But "came into being" is a colorless phrase. The Egyptian interpreted it in terms of begetting and conceiving, and that is natural enough, since he knew the universe to be alive. Hence we meet the strikingly concrete image of the creator who was

joining his seed with his body, to create his egg within his secret self.[15]

This conception of the creator as the absolute origin of all does not by any means render the whole truth about the sun. It ignores the rhythm of its daily rising which dominates man's life. The sun was reborn every dawn; Nut, the sky, or Hathor, the primeval image of the mother as a cow, brought him forth. Hence the following phrase in the morning-hymns:

Hail to thee, Great One, who came forth from the Heavenly Cow.

Or:

Thy mother Nut has borne thee.
How beautiful art thou, Re-Harakhte.

This view and the one that the sun was the creator who, in so far as he could be said to have an origin at all, had

---

[13] After Günther Roeder, *Urkunden zur Religion des alten Ägypten* (Jena, 1915), p. 108.
[14] After Alexander Scharff, *Aegyptische Sonnenlieder* (Berlin, 1922).
[15] Alan H. Gardiner, "Hymns to Amon from a Leiden Papyrus," in *Zeitschrift für aegyptische Sprache*, 42 (1905), 25.

made himself—these two views are found side by side in the same hymns. In the sun-hymn of King Haremhab, for instance, we read:

All praise thee when thou risest radiantly at the horizon.
Thou art beautiful and young as the sun disk in the arms of thy
  mother Hathor.

But a few lines further:

> Thou art a divine youth, the heir of eternity,
> Who begot thyself and bore thyself.

Here then we find an abrupt juxtaposition of views which we should consider mutually exclusive. This is what I have called a multiplicity of approaches: the avenue of preoccupation with life and death leads to one imaginative conception, that with the origin of the existing world to another. Each image, each concept was valid within its own context. There are more to be found in connection with the sun. For instance, his risings could be viewed as a victory over the powers of darkness which were also the powers of death, and when the emphasis fell upon the triumphal character of the sun, his rising was not viewed as due to a passive undergoing of rebirth but as a battle maintained by the sun standing in his boat and sailing through the sky by day and through the underworld by night (Figure 8). His boat is then manned by allied gods and the enemy is Apophis, the serpent or dragon of darkness. In Haremhab's hymn, from which we have quoted already, this aspect of the sun is invoked when he is addressed as

Lord of Eternity within thy ship.[16]

---

[16] This and the preceding quotations are after Scharff, *Aegyptische Sonnenlieder.*

Not only in the texts, but also in their art, the Egyptians combined the different conceptions which we have discussed. In the tomb of Seti I at Thebes, the Heavenly Cow is depicted supported by Shu, the air (Figure 9). But the sun is shown, not as Hathor's calf, but in his boat sailing along the cow's body. In the cenotaph of the same king at Abydos, there is a different rendering (Figure 10): the sky appears as a woman bending over the earth with Shu's support. She has borne the sun, who has fallen at her feet (as a disk indicates) only to take wing again as a beetle. The beetle was believed to create itself in the earth and was therefore a fitting symbol for a self-created god, but hardly for the child of the sky-goddess. And yet such quasi-conflicting images, whether encountered in paintings or in texts, should not be dismissed in the usual derogatory manner. They display a meaningful inconsistency, and not poverty but superabundance of imagination. If we see in them failures, proof of the Egyptians' inability to achieve intellectual synthesis, we simply misconstrue their purpose. The Egyptians exalted their gods by dwelling on the infinite complexity of divine power. The hymns and designs must be read as the reiterated statement: "This also can truly be said of thee." I do not deny that this attitude implies a certain intellectual resignation; but this feature is counterbalanced by an unusual reverence for the concrete phenomena, a reverence not unlike that which we observed when discussing the worship of animals. In Egypt all divine power was immanent power.

This discussion of the multiplicity of approaches to a single cosmic god requires a complement; we must consider the converse situation in which one single problem is correlated with several natural phenomena. We might call it a "multiplicity of answers." As an example we shall take the problem of creation, of the origin of existence. In Egypt this was not an intellectual problem in the first place. On the contrary, it was most closely related to the actuality of man's existence, since the universe in which he lived had gone forth, complete and unchangeable, from its maker. Several gods were named as the primary source of existence. At Memphis, Ptah, the power in the earth, was the creator. At Heliopolis and Hermopolis it was the power in the sun, and at Elephantine it was said that Khnum, who appeared as a ram, had made all living beings on a potter's wheel, a detail which remains an enigma. The Egyptians did not consider these views entirely incompatible. Khnum, for instance, was often "identified" with Re, as the modern phrase has it. This identification meant, in reality, that the creative power of Khnum—perhaps originally the symbol of the procreative power of the animal kingdom—was but another manifestation of the power which was normally recognized in the sun. This was expressed by calling the god Khnum-Re. The creation story concerned with Ptah in the Memphite Theology describes how all that exists came into being as the uttered thought, the spoken word, of Ptah; but in thus asserting the supremacy of the earth-god it makes extensive use of images and thoughts evolved in the sun-cults of Heliopolis and Hermopolis.

It is usual to call such combinations syncretistic, but the idea of conflict implied in that term is misleading. It is true that we find in texts of secondary importance a mechanical combination of incompatibles. It is true that even the Memphite Theology, when it calls Ptah *Ta tjenen*, "The Risen Land," introduces the notion of the primeval

hill emerging from the ocean of chaos, and that it thus
uses a feature belonging originally to a solar myth. But it
does so because the notion of a piece of land which rose
up in the watery wastes gave articulation to the Memphite
belief that the earth's power is primary power and hence
the source of all existence. The Memphite Theology cannot be said to achieve a synthesis since it admitted only
selected elements from the solar mythology. But at least it
shows very clearly that the multiplicity of approaches and
of answers did not destroy that elusive entity, Egyptian
religion. The different correlations of phenomena and problems were championed by distinct schools of thought, but
these had much in common at all times. Theologians
might discuss whether the power in the earth or the power
in the sun, or the generative force of living creatures such
as Khnum, was primary power; the fact that creative power
was manifest in every one of these phenomena was not
contested at any point. Many of the modern discussions of
the so-called "syncretism" in Egyptian religion proceed as
if certain localities in Egypt worshiped a single god. This,
of course, was nowhere the case. Even if towns and prov-
inces chose one deity as their emblem, or declared Ptah or
Khnum supreme, the germs of numerous cults were present
everywhere. Many of these were more or less explicitly
adhered to throughout the land. These common cults—
of the sun, of the falcon, of cattle—represent, in the field
of religion, the unity of the Egyptians, which is equally
tangible in the fields of linguistics, archaeology, and physical anthropology. Thus the teachings of the great theological centers presented, to the country at large, not alien
doctrines but clarified insights in which the potentialities
latent throughout Egyptian polytheism were realized.

This more than local, this really nation-wide foundation of advanced theological thought is especially clear
in the rise of the supreme god of the Egyptian Empire,
Amon-Re.[17] Its premise is a multiplicity of answers: the
air no less than the sun was seen to exemplify creative
power. Thebes, the capital of the empire, from time immemorial had worshiped the god Amon, the "Hidden One,"
manifest in the wind which "bloweth where it listeth, and
thou hearest the sound thereof, but canst not tell whence
it cometh, and whither it goeth." But Amon, the wind, was
also, as breath, the mysterious source of life in man and
beast. Now the Thebans, in common with all Egyptians,
acknowledged the power in the sun, the god Re. And in
the second millennium B.C. the belief spread that this god
who ruled the days and the seasons and Amon, the "Hidden One," were one and the same, Amon-Re. The validity
of two traditional answers to the question as to where lay
the source of existence was not impaired, but the recognition that the two answers were identical, that the creative power of air and the creative power in the sun were
one, was more fruitful than any line of thought followed
in former times. If this was syncretism, it was also the
closest approach to the worship of a supreme and universal god known within the scope of Egyptian polytheism.
The hymns which express the new insight are most impressive and make the usual "explanation" of the rise of
Amon-Re as a result of political factors seem singularly
irrelevant.

[17] The god has been made the subject of a profound study: K. Sethe, *Amun
und die acht Urgötter von Hermopolis, Abhandlungen der preussischen
Akademie der Wissenschaften*, phil.-hist. Klasse (Berlin, 1929).

THE IMMANENCE OF THE GODS AND
THE LIMITATIONS OF EGYPTIAN RELIGIOSITY

But Amon-Re, though he was a supreme god, remained immanent in nature. To him was said:

Thine is what thou seest as light, what thou passest through as wind.

There is only one Egyptian dogma which clearly recognizes divinity beyond, not in, the phenomena. In the Memphite Theology,[18] which proclaims Ptah, the earth-god, the primary source of existence, creation is viewed as a spiritual act. Ptah thought—"in his heart," as the Egyptians say—everything that exists, and the utterance of his thought was the creative word that made his thought materialize. Each thing was first a divine thought, then a divine word:

Every divine word came into being through that which was thought by the heart and commanded by the tongue.

And so all that exists is but the objectivated thought of the creator. Moreover, all that exists continues to function through Ptah who dominates the very mechanics of life:

It happened that heart and tongue prevailed over all other members, considering that he (Ptah) is as heart in every body, as tongue in every mouth, of all gods, people, beasts, crawling creatures, and whatever else lives, while he thinks as heart and commands as tongue everything that he wishes. . . .

[18] K. Sethe, *Dramatische Texte zu altaegyptischen Mysterienspielen* (Leipzig, 1928); English translations of large sections of the Memphite Theology are given in Chapter 2 of my *Kingship and the Gods* (Chicago, 1948).

And so justice is done to him who does what is liked, and evil is done to him who does what is hated.

And so life is given to the peaceful, death to the criminal.

And so are done all labor and all arts, the action of the arms, the going of the legs, the movement of all members, according to the command which was thought by the heart and issued by the tongue and which constitutes the significance of all things.

The significance of all things is, then, the divine command that constituted them. And this divine command was not merely concerned with generalities; it had established the world in all its features, once and for all:

He created the local gods, he made the cities, he founded the provincial divisions; he put the gods in their places of worship, he fixed their offerings, he founded their chapels. He made their bodies (statues) resemble that which pleased their hearts (that is, the forms in which they desired to be manifest). And so the gods entered into their bodies of every kind of wood, of every kind of stone, of every kind of clay, of every kind of thing which grows upon him, in which they have taken form.

In the last sentence, and here alone, we get a reminder that Ptah is the power in the earth. The wood, stone, and other materials of which the statues are made, are said to "grow" upon him. But this is a very tenuous link between the story of creation as related in the Memphite Theology and a natural phenomenon, in this case the earth and its fertility. Ptah as creator appears as a transcendent, not an immanent, power, and it is significant that the Memphite doctrine did not find nation-wide adherence as did that which centered on Amon-Re, immanent in sun and wind. The Memphite Theology possessed a degree of abstraction in which the Egyptians were not prepared to acquiesce.

The exactly opposite extreme, which was equally un-acceptable to them, is represented by the sun-cult of Akhenaten.[19] His god was the Aten, the disk of the sun, the actual heavenly body before everyone's eyes, not conceived, of course, as a purely physical phenomenon, since such a conception was simply unknown to the ancients. Nevertheless the Aten was more concrete, less spiritualized through mythology than any other god of Egypt. All the correlations of the sun which we have discussed retained their validity for Akhenaten; but the conception of immanence prevailed strongly over every other aspect of divine power. Akhenaten adored but one power and refused to accept a multiplicity of answers and, again, the Egyptians did not acquiesce. His monotheistic zeal offended their reverence for the phenomena and the tolerant wisdom with which they had done justice to the many-sidedness of reality. Akhenaten's doctrine was execrated and forgotten a few years after his death.

The Memphite Theology and the Aten cult may be said to define the limits of Egyptian religious feeling which would brook no interference with two basic truths: that there were many gods and that they were immanent in nature. Only on this basis could the Egyptians combine a profound awareness of the complexity of the phenomenal world with that of a mystic bond uniting man and nature. But to us the immanence of the gods limits their scope; they appear captives of their own spheres of manifestation.

The Egyptian gods are imperfect as individuals. If we compare two of them—say, Min and Sobek—we find, not two personages, but two sets of functions and emblems.

[19] For the sun cult of Akhenaten see J. H. Breasted, *History of Egypt* (New York, 1912), Ch. XVIII; J. D. S. Pendlebury, *Tell el-Amarna* (London, 1935); Georg Steindorff and Keith C. Seele, *When Egypt Ruled the East* (Chicago, 1942), Ch. XIV.

Min was depicted as an ithyphallic man; he personified the generative force of nature. Sobek was manifest in the crocodile and represented the power of the Nile to rise and fertilize the land. But the hymns and prayers [20] addressed to these gods differ only in the epithets and attributes used. There is no hint that the hymns were addressed to individuals differing in character. This vagueness in the characterization of Egyptian gods stands out most clearly if we compare them with the gods of Sumer. Professor Thorkild Jacobsen has shown recently [21] that these gods retain the grandeur of cosmic powers in texts which yet succeed in describing them as fully developed and coherent characters. Enlil, the god manifest in the storm, appears in the myths as violent, impulsive, and incalculable. Ea, the god manifest in water, appears cunning and helpful. The only comparable individuality among the Egyptian gods is Isis, but she is exceptional. An excellent example of a god who, even conceived in the most lofty manner, retains his character of immanence, is Amon-Re. His elevation to a supreme and universal god was based on the realization that no power in the universe matched the combined significance of sun and air. The Egyptians did not see in Amon-Re —as the Greeks saw in Zeus and the Hebrews in Jahweh —a divinity of so exalted a character that man's relationship with him necessarily became unique. We read in an Amon hymn:

Re himself is united with his body. . . . He is the Universal Lord, beginning of existing things. . . . No gods know his true shape. . . . No witness is borne to him. He is too mysterious

---

[20] Min and Sobek hymns in Roeder, *Urkunden zur Religion des alten Ägypten.*
[21] *The Intellectual Adventure of Ancient Man*, Ch. V.

for his glory to be revealed, too great for question to be asked of him, too powerful to be known.[22]

This is but a small fragment from a long poem which expresses magnificently the feeling of religious awe. But it differs in spirit from certain hymns to Zeus as well as from the Hebrew psalms. Amon-Re's all-pervading power is described as follows:

He lives in what Shu uplifts (the clouds) to the end of the circuit of the sky. He enters into all trees and they become animated, with branches waving . . . He raises heaven to furor and the sea to revolt, and they become peaceful [again] when he comes to peace. He brings the divine Nile to a flood when his heart suggests it. . . . One hears his voice but he is not seen while he lets all throats breathe. He strengthens the heart of her who is in labor and lets the child which comes forth from her live.[23]

There are phrases here, as in previous quotations, which recall the Old Testament. But let us remember how Jahweh made himself known to Elijah (I Kings 19:11–12):

And, behold, the Lord passed by, and a great and strong wind rent the mountains, and brake in pieces the rocks before the Lord; but the Lord was not in the wind: and after the wind an earthquake; but the Lord was not in the earthquake:

And after the earthquake a fire; but the Lord was not in the fire; and after the fire a still small voice.

Inevitably our attention remains fixed on the moving epiphany in the last verse. But we should not overlook the great significance of the introductory negations. Jahweh was not in any natural phenomenon, however majestic it might be. But of Amon-Re it was said: "He lives in

[22] After Gardiner, "Hymns to Amon," p. 34.
[23] After K. Sethe, *Amun und die acht Urgötter.*

what Shu uplifts" and heaven and sea "become peaceful again when he comes to peace."

This comparison should elucidate what I meant when I said that the Egyptian gods seem captives within their own manifestations. They personify power but remain incomplete as personages. And yet these vague and grandiose gods were not distant and intangible; the Egyptian lived forever within the sphere of their activities. Moreover, he comprehended these activities to a large extent in terms of human existence. This is a common feature in polytheism. For if the universe is animated, it is best understood in terms of human life. We have seen that the Egyptians explained the daily appearance of the sun as its birth; the moon waned because it was the ailing eye of Horus. When barley was made into beer and bread, it was Osiris—manifest in the grain—who died. We shall meet such images at every turn, and we must not interpret them as allegories, for we cannot abstract a meaning from them without falsifying the beliefs which they express. Images are not ornaments or adjuncts of ancient thought. They are inseparable from it because the ancients reached their insight in a manner which was intuitive and imaginative as much as intellectual.

The irreducible unity of image and thought is but another aspect of the correlations which we have discussed in connection with Isis and with the cosmic gods. It is most clearly illustrated by the Egyptian beliefs in immortality, which we shall discuss in Chapter 4 below. When the universe is seen, not as dead matter, but as suffused with life, man's own existence—with the critical phases of birth, procreation, and death—imparts significance to the cosmic phenomena and acquires a new depth in return. When the sunset is inseparable from the thought of death, dawn is a surety of resurrection. In this way the immanence of the gods in nature, far from diminishing their significance for the Egyptians, enabled a correlation of human and natural life which was an inexhaustible source of strength. The life of man, as an individual and even more as a member of society, was integrated with the life of nature, and we shall see in subsequent chapters that the experience of that harmony was thought to be the greatest good to which man could aspire.

2
The Egyptian State

THE Egyptian language lacked a word for "state." It could express "country" in more ways than one, and it could designate foreign peoples. But although Egypt is the oldest example of what Webster calls a "body of people occupying a definite territory and politically organized under one government," this rational definition of the word "state" would have been meaningless to the Egyptians. It would, for one thing, have been too anthropocentric; the Egyptians did not feel that their country was just a piece of land which they happened to occupy. The bond between them and their land was as singular and as strong as the bond of blood, and even political institutions were involved in a feeling of unalterable rightness.

The Egyptian state was not a man-made alternative to other forms of political organization. It was god-given, established when the world was created; and it continued to form part of the universal order. In the person of Pharaoh a superhuman being had taken charge of the affairs of man. And this great blessing, which ensured the well-being of the nation, was not due to a fortunate accident but had been foreseen in the divine plan. The monarchy then was as old as the world, for the creator himself had assumed kingly office on the day of creation. Pharaoh was his descendant and his successor. The word "state" was absent from the language because all the significant aspects of the state were concentrated in the king. He was the fountainhead of all authority, all power, and all wealth. The famous saying of Louis XIV, *l'état c'est moi*, was levity and presumption when it was uttered, but could have been offered by Pharaoh as a statement of fact in which his subjects concurred. It would have summed up adequately their political philosophy.

There can be no doubt about this. The practical organization of the Egyptian commonwealth implies it; the texts and monuments proclaim it; and it is confirmed by the absence of any trace of revolution in three thousand years of recorded history. Pharaoh was no mere despot holding an unwilling people in slavery. He ruled in the strictest sense by divine right; and any attempt to describe the Egyptian state irrespective of the doctrine of Pharaoh's divinity would be fatuous. We might as well discuss a modern democracy without reference to the doctrine of the freedom and equality of men. We know how thoroughly this last doctrine has molded our mores and institutions; we shall see that the belief in the divinity of their king similarly affected the everyday life of the Egyptians.

We must, then, face the fact that a basic conviction of the Egyptians is totally alien to us. But we cannot evade that difficulty, least of all by quasi-rational interpretations. The doctrine of the divinity of kings has been viewed as a consequence of a misunderstanding—a metaphor taken literally—or as an elaborate fraud by men in power anxious to secure its continuation by sanctifying it. Similar pseudo-explanations have been rejected by historians and anthropologists alike, and the facts we are about to discuss will once more expose their shallowness. The doctrine of divine kingship is only comparable to a religious creed. It carries conviction beyond dispute, fulfills emotional needs, and may give rise, as we shall see, to moral and intellectual considerations of a high order.

I have discussed divine kingship elsewhere in detail, and we shall consider it here only in so far as is necessary for an understanding of the Egyptian state. Moreover, we shall concentrate on the features which are at all times characteristic of that state, since a discussion of historical changes would take us too far and would not throw light on the fundamental conception. The same applies to the problem of origin; we shall not discuss how the Egyptian monarchy as we know it came into being. This, too, I have done elsewhere, but it remains a matter of conjecture, since even the earliest texts and monuments take the rule of a divine king for granted. We observe that the monarchy was always regarded as the only form of political organization that was conceivable, the realization of a predestined order of society. Apparently it possessed the compelling authority of an answer to an unconscious need, and it must therefore have been in profound harmony with the Egyptian mentality. It is with this in mind that we shall attempt to understand the Egyptian state.

We shall proceed in three stages: First we shall describe the political and economic organization of Egypt in historical times as it is revealed by the documents. It will then appear that the whole apparatus of government was but an implement for the execution of the royal command. We shall, in the second place, consider the omnipotent ruler at the head of the state, and we shall find that his individuality escapes us entirely and in every instance. Even in his lifetime he appears to belong to the sphere of myth as much as to that of actuality. Consequently (and in the third place) we shall have to find an explanation of the political philosophy of the Egyptians in the view they took of the world in general.

THE ORGANIZATION OF THE STATE

The Egyptian state was highly centralized. Many decisions were taken by the king or by his deputy, the vizier, or could be referred back to them, but the business of government was actually carried on by a vast body of officials. The social status of these men differed in different periods, but we can disregard these details here. Only the situation prevailing during the early part of the Old Kingdom is illuminating. At that time we find "royal kinsmen" throughout the administration. The king's sons or brothers filled the offices of vizier or treasurer or were high priests in the main temples. Descendants of earlier kings or distant relatives got less important appointments down to quite subordinate posts in the provincial administration. The usual view that this system ensured loyalty to the throne is contrary to the observed facts: everywhere and at all times the scions of great houses have caused trouble by becoming pretenders. The preponderance of royal kinsmen in the administration follows from the unique nature of the king. Only those who were of the blood royal—in however slight a degree—were fit to exercise authority, since all authority was delegated royal power.

In later times this system was abandoned. But even when the bureaucracy had no connection with the royal house, it remained a structure based on delegated personal power. This explains the fact that judicial and executive functions were often combined: "The courts of law consisted of meetings of the local dignitaries under the chairmanship of an official who presided over the trial."[1] The courts in descending order were Pharaoh, the vizier, the governor of a province, the local authorities. As regards the last, one sometimes reads a few names of judges with the addition, "the whole group of laborers," as if an unspecified number of local worthies could take part.[2] The vizier was chief justice, in appeal and in first instance, and was assisted by a *Kenbet* or council which probably functioned in an advisory capacity only.[3] Not only were executive and judicial functions combined, but even the competence of the different departments of government was not clearly defined. But this, again, follows from the peculiar nature of their authority; they all acted ultimately as deputies of Pharaoh in whom rested all authority, undifferentiated. A certain amount of specialized departmental training existed, and was encouraged by the practice of having a son succeed to his father's office. The father associated his son as an apprentice and assistant in the expectation that in time he would be allowed to hand over his functions; and thus continuity and efficiency were

[1] E. Seidl, in S. R. K. Glanville, ed., *The Legacy of Egypt* (Oxford, 1942), p. 204, describes this in the New Kingdom, but the "Eloquent Peasant" shows that it was true for earlier times too; Rensi was on his way to such a court, and Uni's appointment to the court of Nekhen, although he was an administrative official, shows the same.

[2] Alexander Scharff and Erwin Seidl, *Einführung in die ägyptische Rechtsgeschichte bis zum Ende des neuen Reiches* in "Ägyptologische Forschungen" (Glückstadt, 1939), Part 10, p. 32, referring to Jacques Pirenne, *Histoire des institutions et du droit privé de l'ancienne Égypte* (Brussells, 1932), I, 73, 274.

[3] The judicial power of officials over their inferiors was stayed in the hall of the vizier, so that an unprejudiced hearing and discussion of the cases of lower officials were possible. See Sethe, *Urkunden des ägyptischen Altertums* (Leipzig, 1909), IV, 1107; Breasted, *Ancient Records of Egypt* (Chicago, 1907), II, § 681.

furthered. But each succession had to be authorized by Pharaoh; for, as the Papyrus of Ani puts it, "offices have no children." At any time the king could—and did—appoint outsiders. In fact, the noteworthy careers, as preserved for us in tomb inscriptions, broke through all departmental limitations. Men of humble origin could rise to the top once their gifts were recognized; and we find that they were called to a succession of posts which would seem to us to have required entirely different preparatory training. For example, in the Sixth Dynasty a certain Uni started as undercustodian of royal domains.[4] Later he obtained court rank and a priestly office—the latter a necessity since courtiers, in contact with the divine king, had to be ritually pure. He was promoted to be a superior custodian of domains and became also judge in the court of Nekhen. When a conspiracy in the royal harem was discovered, the king by-passed the vizier and all other courts and instructed Uni with one assessor to investigate the case in great secrecy. Next Uni was put in command of an army and led five campaigns against the Bedaween in the Sinai Desert, and a campaign in southern Palestine where the troops were transported overseas. Finally he became governor of the South, one of the highest administrative appointments, and was charged in that capacity with the quarrying and transportation of a royal sarcophagus and other tomb fittings in the region of the First Cataract, and with the cutting of canals to improve navigation.

The career of Uni is typical of those of outstanding men in all periods of Egyptian history. Since all authority bore a personal character, officials could be used in whatever function seemed desirable at any moment. But the con-

[4] Breasted, *Ancient Records* I, §§ 291–94, 306–15, 319–24.

comitant fluidity of competence, even between departments, was a source of confusion. This is illustrated, for instance, by a set of letters from Ramessid times which have come down to us.[5] We read that a scribe of the treasury, attempting to collect the balance of a shipment of textiles, was confronted by a steward who claimed the goods as due his own branch of the civil service. The steward had the scribe arrested, and the latter, threatened with physical violence, gave in. In such a case—a conflict within the administration—there was no court competent to adjudicate the matter. The scribe, if he was anxious to save his standing with his superiors, had to sue the steward under what we should call civil law. In this case the steward was personally indicted and made responsible for the return of the textiles to the scribe of the treasury. We see, then, that towards the end of the second millennium, Egypt did not possess a bureaucracy in the modern sense in which a circumscribed function defines the scope of personal initiative. Egyptian officialdom retained at all times and in all its strata the characteristic of personal authority, and that because it devolved ultimately from Pharaoh. This left great scope to energetic individuals; but it depended upon the direction in which they used their gifts, and upon the control exercised at the center of government, whether the opportunity thus offered must be counted an advantage or a drawback.

The people, in so far as they formed no part of the bureaucracy, labored nonetheless in the service of Pharaoh. The villagers could be called up for all kinds of corvée. They were obliged to lodge and feed the messengers who

[5] Adolf Erman and Hermann Ranke, *Aegypten und aegyptisches Leben im Altertum* (Tübingen, 1923), 124.

traveled continuously to and from the capital, and the police, too, who seem to have lived off the land.[6] A proportion of the young men of every hamlet or estate were drafted into the army. But warfare was the least frequent of their occupations. They normally served as a labor corps, assisting in quarrying or building operations, irrigation works, or expeditions to neighboring regions which supplied Egypt with many of its raw materials.

Here we touch upon a function of Pharaoh as momentous as his heading of the administration. The Nile Valley produced foodstuffs in abundance, but almost all other substances had to be obtained from outside. In Mesopotamia, where similar conditions obtained, merchants took charge of the import trade. In Egypt the word for "merchant," *šwy.ty,* is not found before the New Kingdom, and when it occurs it designates the officials of certain temples who had been granted the privilege of foreign trade by the king.[7] The import trade was a royal monopoly, except that this term suggests to us the totally irrelevant conception of a profit-making concern. The king owned all, in any case, and organized the foreign trade to supply the needs of the commonwealth as regards raw materials. Royal expeditions went to mine gold in Nubia; malachite, turquoise, and perhaps copper in Sinai; or stone in the eastern desert. Royal fleets went to Byblos on the Phoenician coast to fetch wood, and through the Red Sea to Punt-Somaliland for frankincense and myrrh. These overseas ventures brought the Egyptians in contact with people of some culture and power who insisted on a *quid pro quo* in their dealings. Hence the Egyptian envoys plied a kind

[6] H. Kees, "Aegypten," in *Kulturgeschichte des alten Orients* (Walter Otto, ed., *Handbuch der Altertumswissenschaft,* München, 1933), p. 46.
[7] Kees, "Aegypten," p. 104, n. 1.

of diplomatic trade; they offered valuable presents to the local rulers, enough perhaps to count as a fair price for their purchases. Objects bearing Pharaoh's name have been found in the tombs of the princes of Byblos, and they belong to the very best which Egyptian jewelers produced.[8] In return for such presents the local princes had trees felled or frankincense heaped on the shore for Pharaoh's envoys to take away and record as tribute on the monuments at home. In Nubia and the eastern desert there were no local princes to deal with. The populations of these regions were ignored, and the expeditions took what they wanted.

These were large-scale undertakings. A treasury official of the Middle Kingdom reports that he transported eighty blocks of stone from the Wady Hammamat in the eastern desert with groups of 1,000, 1,500, and 2,000 men, the blocks being pulled on rollers, in all probability, and that "without a single man getting exhausted, without a man thirsting on the way, without a moment of ill will. On the contrary, the whole army (note this word!) came home in good spirits, sated with bread, drunk with beer, as if it were the beautiful festival of a god." [9] Such "armies," of course, contained craftsmen such as masons and sculptors, but by far the largest number of "soldiers" were ordinary levies who, like the modern fellaheen, supplied labor for any task in hand. Sometimes an expedition fulfilled a multiple purpose. Henu, another official of the treasury, went with 3,000 men through the Wady Hammamat to the Red Sea, carrying wood to build a seagoing ship on the Red Sea coast for a trip to Punt in search of frankincense; on

[8] P. Montet, *Byblos et l'Egypte* (Paris, 1928–29), Pls. 88–94.
[9] After Kees, "Aegypten," pp. 139–41.

the way there he reconditioned the wells along the route, on the way back he quarried and brought stone with him.[10]

The king alone could command that undertakings of this magnitude be set on foot. Hence we find that tombs built of quarried stone are often gifts from the ruler to certain courtiers and officials, while others received only a sculptured slab or niche and the actual tomb had to be built, generally of sun-dried brick, by labor available to the recipient in his official function or on his estate.

The expeditions to the south, to Nubia, mined gold and requisitioned or bartered cattle, panther skins, ostrich feathers, ivory, and so on. A frontier stela erected by Senusert III forbade any Negro to pass beyond it, either by ship or on foot or driving cattle, unless he was on his way to barter his goods at a near-by emporium. The imported goods were mostly essential commodities and their distribution was largely effected through the king, taking place in the form of grants and as payments for services, all of which were made in goods. Gold, silver, copper, oil, wood, and linen, to name but a few, were turned over to the great officials, who in turn made gifts and payments to their dependents, and so on down the social scale. It is most remarkable that the supply of raw materials, which was dependent on the king's bounty, was sufficient, and that this system did succeed in bringing a great variety of goods into circulation. However, districts not well connected with the capital were apt to be starved for materials. This has been shown by excavations of Qau el Kebir, a small provincial town in Middle Egypt on the eastern, less important, bank of the Nile.[11] During the

10 *Ibid.*, p. 123.
11 Guy Brunton, *Qau and Badari* (London, 1927), I, 75.

flourishing period of the Old Kingdom, when the pyramids were built and rich tombs were equipped for the king and his officials near Memphis, the graves at Qau el Kebir were of the poorest. But after the collapse of the central government, in the First Intermediate period, the effective power was in the hands of the local dignitaries (page 84 below). The tombs near the capital were very poorly supplied with grave goods at that time, but those at Qau were now for the first time equipped with alabaster vases, jewelry of semiprecious stone, and even gold. It is equally significant that at this time men were buried with their weapons. This had not been usual hitherto, but a contemporary text states that "a man goes ploughing carrying his shield." [12]

In normal times, then, private trade on a large scale did not exist. There was, of course, extensive barter in local markets, where products of home industries, surplus crops, birds and fishes caught in the marshes, implements and such valuables as had reached the populace, changed hands. Such markets are repeatedly depicted in the tombs. In one case [13] one sees Phoenician merchantmen just made fast to the quay at Thebes, while local vendors sit in their booths offering refreshments, sandals, and similar articles, waiting for the crews to disembark. The standards of value were fixed weights of gold, silver, or copper. Free enterprise did exist but it remained, as it were, marginal. The economy of the country as a whole was dependent on the distribution of raw materials and produce through the king's agents. This applies not only to importations but,

[12] After Adolf Erman, *The Literature of the Ancient Egyptians,* tr. A. M. Blackman (London, 1927), p. 94.
[13] *Revue archéologique,* II (1898), Pl. 15.

to an even larger extent, to barley, emmer, cattle, wine, linen, and other native produce. These goods were turned over by the royal storehouses as wages and salaries to artisans, officials, artists, priests, and others not directly engaged in food production. They were collected from the farms and the large estates (including the temple estates) in the form of taxes. Here again the distribution of goods was a function of Pharaoh, and this was expressed by the Egyptians in the simple statement that Pharaoh owned the land.

Since land was the basis of taxation its distribution was a matter of great concern. Private ownership was acknowledged in practice, but in theory it was viewed as a royal grant which could be revoked at any moment. A cadaster was kept at the office of the vizier, and all transactions concerning land had to be recorded and authenticated there. We read, for instance, in an Old Kingdom text:

Him were given 50 aruras of land, from his mother's estate, when she made out a will for her children. It was handed over to them by royal decree.[14]

Litigations concerning land were heard by the vizier in person; he also had to give permission for the cutting down of trees, always rare and valuable in Egypt. Trees, ponds, canals, and wells were taxed, as well as all herds and flocks and the yield of chase and fishery.[15] The main source of taxes was the harvest, which was calculated on the height of the inundation recorded annually at least since the First Dynasty. Seed corn was advanced to the

[14] After Sethe, *Urkunden*, I, 2; Kees, "Aegypten," p. 44, n. 6.
[15] Kees, "Aegypten," pp. 39–40. The whole section on the rural economies of Egypt (pp. 18–53) is outstandingly good.

peasant, and oxen for ploughing were let out to him. Then, at harvest time, officials of the treasury, accompanied by scribes and by policemen carrying sticks, came to take what was due to the royal storehouses, whence it reached all those who were directly or indirectly dependent on Pharaoh for their sustenance. Thus the Egyptian, whether he was part of the official hierarchy or not, was entirely subservient to the state as personified in Pharaoh. In Max Weber's words: "Everyone was tied to the function which he exercised within the social organism; in principle no one was free." [16]

Weber's statement correctly links the absence of personal freedom—the correlate of the king's absolute power —with the function of each individual in the community. For not even the most superficial observer can conclude that the people and the land with its resources were merely at the service of the king's pleasure. Our summary description of the Egyptian state indicates that Pharaoh fulfilled an indispensable function: his personal power appears as the integrating factor of the body politic. It became effective through a corps of officials functioning exclusively by virtue of his delegation of authority. Royal enterprises supplied all the needs of the community which native produce could not satisfy; moreover, the distribution of the native produce was effected through the king's agency. The state was for the Egyptian simply the sphere of the king's activity; hence a civilized, orderly existence was dependent on the king.

The premises of Pharaoh's great personal power lie in the religious implications of Egyptian kingship. These

[16] Max Weber, *Gesammelte Aufsätze zur Sozial- und Wirtschaftsgeschichte* (Tübingen, 1924), p. 65.

were succinctly expressed when the vizier Rekhmire
wrote in his tomb:

What is the king of Upper and Lower Egypt? He is a god by
whose dealings one lives, the father and the mother of all men,
alone by himself without an equal.[17]

"A god by whose dealings one lives"—that is the function of Pharaoh as the Egyptians saw it. And so we may
understand that they did not consider their condition as
a state of intolerable slavery. The total absence of popular risings would otherwise be inexplicable. We know of
troubles when the administrative machinery broke down;
there were, for instance, strikes and demonstrations in
the Theban necropolis in Ramessid times when rations
fell a month behind time.[18] But there is no trace of any
political movement against the existing order. On the
contrary, the people showed their affection for the insti-
tution of kingship by placing it in the center of their en-
tertainment literature. The literary works, too, are all concerned with the king but it is more significant that tales,
which by their artless form and coarse humor are clearly
marked as products of the story-teller in the market place,
dwell on the king and his court with the greatest insistence, and cast even myths about the gods in the form of
court chronicles.

For the king's power, though absolute, was not arbitrary. Pharaoh championed justice, *Maat*. In fact, the
king was the fount of justice as he was the source of all
authority; it is most significant that we have no indis-

[17] After Alan H. Gardiner, "The Autobiography of Rekhmire," in *Zeitschrift
für aegyptische Sprache*, 60 (1925), 69.
[18] Adolf Erman and Hermann Ranke, *Aegypten und aegyptisches Leben
im Altertum* (Tübingen, 1923), pp. 140–41.

putable evidence of the existence of codified law from Egypt. On the other hand, a short quotation from a law in a papyrus of the Twentieth Dynasty [19] takes the following significant form: "Pharaoh has said, Let every woman's dowry(?) be given to her." And in the Edict of King Haremhab [20] the king describes, not any study of existing legislation, but how he "took counsel with his heart how he might expel evil and suppress untruth," and then presents his enactments, again without any reference to prevailing codes, but in the following form: (1) statement that a certain type of abuse exists and that this displeases the king; (2) a conditional phrase: If henceforth such-and-such a wrong is committed; (3) statement as to what penalty the king desires to be inflicted in the case.

In theory every subject had access to Pharaoh for petitioning and every dispute could be submitted to his inspired and *ipso facto* just decision. The king's deputy and chief justice, the vizier, was explicitly instructed at his investiture to receive any petitioner; the emphasis with which his "instructions" insist on the duty of being just contrasts sharply with the lack of other specific directives. I quote Professor Seele's translation:

Look after the office of the vizier and watch over everything that is done in it, for it is the constitution of the entire land. As to the office of the vizier, indeed, it is not pleasant; no, it is as bitter as its reputation. . . . He is one who must give no special consideration to princes or councilors nor make slaves of any people whatsoever. . . . Look upon him whom you know as on him whom you do not know, the one who approaches your person

[19] J. Černý and T. Eric Peet, in *Journal of Egyptian Archaeology,* XIII (1927), 33 (Turin Papyrus 2021: 3, 4).
[20] K. Pflüger, in *Journal of Near Eastern Studies,* V (1946), 260–68; Breasted, *Ancient Records,* III, §§ 45–67.

as the one who is far from your house. . . . Pass over no petitioner without hearing his case. . . . Show anger to no man
wrongfully and be angry only at that which deserves anger.
Instil fear of yourself that you may be held in fear, for a true
prince is a prince who is feared. The distinction of a prince is
that he does justice. But if a man instils fear in an excessive
manner, there being in him a modicum of injustice in the esti-
mation of men, they do not say of him: That is a just man. . . .
What one expects of the conduct of the vizier is the performance
of justice.[21]

There is reason to believe that these injunctions did not
remain empty phrases. The service of Pharaoh was a religious, not a purely secular, function, and sense of duty
was strengthened by faith. Funerary texts like that of
Pepinakht (page 82 below) confirm this. The instructions
themselves refer to a vizier who on principle decided against
his relatives lawsuits involving members of his family. The
grim virtue of such an attitude shows how seriously the officials took their duty to be just. But it is characteristic of the
Egyptians that the "instructions" warn the vizier not to
follow this example, with the addition: "For this is more
than justice." Equally revealing are certain phrases in
tomb inscriptions which go beyond the enunciation of
generalities. Harkhuf, governor of the South, states, for
instance: "Never did I judge two brothers in such a way
that a son was deprived of his paternal possession." [22]

There are plenty of Egyptian letters and other documents that mention abuse of power, but one gets the impression that the culprits are, on the whole, lesser officials
and that the men in responsible positions acted with fair-
ness and dignity. That appears, for instance, in the "Tale

[21] After Georg Steindorff and Keith C. Seele, *When Egypt Ruled the
East* (Chicago, 1942), p. 87.
[22] After Breasted, *Ancient Records*, I, § 331.

of the Eloquent Peasant," which we shall discuss later
(page 146 and following). The peasant, robbed and bullied
by an underling of the high steward Rensi, presents his
case to that high official, who retains a disapproving silence when some colleagues of the evildoer insist that one
should not take the complaints of a poor farmer too seriously. The peasant, for his part, insists in no uncertain
terms on his right to receive justice, and in doing so refers
explicitly to the king as the guarantor of justice. For instance, he says to the high steward: "Do justice for the
Lord of Justice," [23] and again: "The king is indoors, the
rudder is in *thy* hand; and trouble is spread in thy vicinity.
. . . Let thy tongue be directed aright, do not stray
away." [24] These are not words normally spoken by the subjects of a tyrant. But the conviction which supports the
words, namely, that justice is of the essence of government,
inseparable from the king, and hence the acknowledged
object of an official's concern, is founded on a conception
of justice which pertains not only to ethics, but also to
metaphysics. We cannot discuss this conception of justice, *Maat*, before we have clarified the Egyptians' conception of Pharaoh.

THE PERSON OF THE MONARCH

The Egyptian monuments and texts have been a disap-
pointment to historians in that they consistently hide the
individuality of the kings under generalities. The rulers
in whose name every act of government was undertaken,
who erected vast monuments and prided themselves on
great deeds, remain totally impersonal to us. Some few dis-

[23] After Gardiner, in *Journal of Egyptian Archaeology,* IX (1923), 19.
[24] *Ibid.*, pp. 12–13. Italics mine.

tinctive features, which were long believed to be individual traits (such as the initiative and courage of Tuthmosis III at the battle of Megiddo), have since been recognized as conventional elements in the portrait of an ideal ruler.[25] The texts present us throughout with the traditional conception of the king, and the sculptures present us, similarly, with ideals, not with portraits. The differences between the royal heads are largely those of period, because the ideals—or, rather, specific details in the lasting ideal of kingship—changed somewhat in the course of time. We can distinguish the serene and abundant vigor of Old Kingdom sculptures, the proud and somber spiritual strength of the Middle Kingdom, and the refined steely force of the New Kingdom; we can distinguish more finely between, say, the spontaneity in the early part of the New Kingdom and the sophistication noticeable towards its end. We can sometimes formulate the distinctive features of works belonging to a single reign; but we are rarely convinced that a given work reveals the personal character of the king whom it depicts. At most we recognize that a distinctive physiognomy is allowed to modify the ideal image somewhat. This individualization is imposed upon a basic ideal of kingship which was rendered in a form characteristic for the time in which the statue was made. Uninscribed statues can almost always be assigned to a given period, hardly ever with certainty to an individual ruler.

The prevalence of typical over individual features in the literary and plastic monuments accentuates once more the gulf which separates Pharaoh from the despot bent on

[25] A. de Buck, *Het Typische en het Individueele bij de Egyptenaren* (Leiden, 1929).

personal power and aggrandizement. The almost omnipotent rulers of Egypt were satisfied, in contrast with the
tyrants of all ages, to let their individuality merge with the
impersonal portrait of the ideal ruler. Even in the accounts of royal achievements which we should classify as
historical texts, we find, to our exasperation, that everything that is singular and historical is treated as of little
account. For example, we find that King Pepi II depicted
his victory over the Libyans with such apparent care that
he even had the names of captured Libyan chiefs written
beside their images in the reliefs of his temple. But we
happen to know that captured Libyan chiefs with precisely
the same names figure in the reliefs of King Sahure, two
hundred years earlier! In the same way Ramses III enu-
merated his conquests in Asia by name, but in so doing
copied a list of Ramses II, who, in his turn, had utilized a
list of Tuthmosis III.

We obviously miss the point entirely if we pretend to
"explain" such usages by an appeal to the carelessness of
designers or the vanity of their masters. None of these
rulers stood in need of borrowing; their own achievements
were considerable. But there was no reason why their
draftsmen should not copy what was at hand on extant
monuments. The identity of the king's enemies changed,
of course, from generation to generation, but for this very
reason it was devoid of all real interest. The enemies were
sufficiently identified by a conventional term, the "Nine
Bows" (Figure 18). When depicted, these included all
Egypt's neighbors: the Negroes of the South, the Libyans
of the West, the Asiatics of the East. It was understood that
Pharaoh was victor over all of them. One might elaborate
the theme and render enemies actually defeated in the

reign of a given king; but such historical details, which for us would form the quintessence, were for the Egyptians mere embellishment of text or design. For real importance attached only to the perennial truth that Pharaoh ruled supreme among all men. The usual pictorial renderings of Pharaoh's victories represent this unchanging truth and are therefore conventional. From the First Dynasty onward a gigantic figure of Pharaoh was shown destroying one or more defeated enemies (Figure 15). Place names, if they occur at all (as they do on the right in our figure), form a decorative fringe to the design; the reliefs, like the texts, emphasize the traditional, at the expense of the historical elements of the victory. The army is not depicted before the Nineteenth Dynasty, and then only in a subsidiary position (Figure 16); the king continues to appear as the fountainhead of all effective action, as the sole agent of victory. But in victory, as in every other deed of his reign, the king acts out and realizes a prefigured course of events.

CHANGE, PERMANENCE, AND
THE CONCEPTION OF MAAT

We touch here on a fundamental feature of Egyptian kingship, a feature rooted deeply in the Egyptian mentality: the touchstone for all that was really significant was its permanence. That was important which had always been and would never change. To say that the Egyptians held this view does not amount to calling them traditionalists. Their conviction went deeper than a reverence for traditional values. It derived from an attitude of mind which comprehended the universe as essentially static. Movement and change were not denied to exist, of course; but change, in so far as it was significant, was recurrent change, the life rhythm of a universe which had gone forth, complete and unchanging, from the hands of its creator. The alternation of night and day, of drought and inundation, of the succession of the seasons, were significant changes; their movement was part of the established order of creation. But single occurrences, odd events, historical circumstances were ephemeral, superficial disturbances of the regularity of being and for that reason unimportant.

It is clear that people holding such views could not be deeply interested in historical detail when they erected monuments commemorating victories of their rulers; such details were no more than the accidental setting in which an unchanging truth had become manifest on a particular occasion. What mattered was the nature of Pharaoh's rulership, which was such as to doom every opposition. For his authority was founded not in the social, but in the cosmic order. Kingship, in Egypt, was as old as the world. It dated from the day of creation.

We must for a moment consider this connection of kingship with creation—"the first time," as the Egyptians called it—a little more closely. References to the creation turn up with great frequency in Egyptian texts; a large number of creation stories were current; to all appearances, the concept played a very much larger part in Egyptian thought than in that of most other peoples. This is due to the Egyptians' view of the world. In a static world, creation is the only event that really matters supremely, since it alone can be said to have made a change. It makes the difference between the nothingness of chaos and the fullness of the present which has emerged as a result of that unique act. Consequently the story of the creation held the clue to the understanding of the present and it was for this reason that accounts of the creation were commented upon and elaborated with unvarying interest. They did not merely satisfy intellectual curiosity; they did not merely answer the theoretical question how things came into being; they did not even serve—as such accounts do in the Psalms and the Book of Job—to magnify God by extolling his first and most astounding manifestation of power. In Egypt the creation stories displayed, with a clarity which actual conditions often lacked, the articulation of the existing order and the interrelation and significance of its component parts.

The social order was part of the cosmic order. All theological schools agreed that kingship, the pivot of society, belonged to the basic order of existence and had been introduced at the time of creation. We quoted in the preceding chapter a text describing how Ptah made the local gods, the cities, and in fact the whole order of existence. This passage ends with the following line which simply assigns to Ptah the title of king of Egypt:

Thus all the gods are at one with him (Ptah), content and united with the Lord of the Two Lands.

We saw also that it was more commonly the sun-god who counted as the creator in Egypt, and that it is therefore the sun, Re, who is called the first king of Egypt. This happens not only in religious texts, but also—significantly—in *historical* documents, like the king list of the Turin Papyrus of the second millennium B.C. or the history of the Ptolemaic priest Manetho. In a hymn the sun-god is even addressed as if he were a *dead* king:

King Re, of blessed memory, sovereign of the Two Lands,
Tremendous in strength, rich in power,
All highest, who made the whole earth.[26]

This treatment of the sun-god is unusual. I have translated a little freely to indicate, by the term "of blessed
memory," that Re is here regarded as a power of the past.
But as a rule the Egyptians were very much aware of the
sun as a living power; and they held, therefore, that he
had disposed of his rulership of Egypt by handing it over
to other gods; in the end it fell to the god Horus, who was
incarnate in each Pharaoh. This delegation of power, far
from removing Pharaoh from the divine sphere, put him,
on the contrary, on a par with other gods. These, too, were
children of the creator; for when the universe is alive, creation is conceived as procreation. Now to say that the creator first brought Shu and Tefnut (air and moisture) into
existence, and that these in turn brought forth Geb and Nut
(earth and sky) is to express, with all the concreteness of
mythopoeic thought, the idea that powers latent in the
creator were objectivated as distinct deities who now exercised power in their appropriate spheres. Similarly, kingship, once exercised by the creator, was put in charge of
the deity incarnate in Pharaoh. The kingly character of
the creator is clearly expressed when the "Book of the
Dead" quotes his words and supplies them with an ex-
planatory gloss:

I am Atum when I was alone in Nun (the primeval ocean). I am
Re in his first appearance when he began to rule that which he
had made. (Gloss): What does that mean?—This "Re when he
began to rule that which he had made" means that Re began to

26 After Alexander Scharff, *Aegyptische Sonnenlieder* (Berlin, 1922),
p. 48.

appear *as a king,* as one who existed before Shu had even lifted
heaven from earth.

Thus the whole universe was a monarchy, and the king
of the world had been the first king of Egypt. This function
had devolved upon his son and successor, Pharaoh. But it
had lost nothing of its nature in the transmission. The rule
of Pharaoh still contained an element of creativity; it was
an inspired rule which drew its certainties from sources
beyond human control. Hence the texts abound in expressions which exalt Pharaoh by describing his acts as
reflections, equivalents, and repetitions of those of Re.
Elsewhere I have discussed this parallelism in detail; [27] I
shall quote here only one single instance, which is revealing because it shows how this parallelism has found un-
premeditated expression in certain turns of speech and
usages of orthography. The verb *khay* is written with a
hieroglyph depicting the sun appearing upon the primeval
hill; this hill was the first dry land which Re made in the
waters of chaos so that he might "find a place where he
could stand," as the texts have it. The word *khay* means
"to shine forth," and is used to describe the appearance of
the sun at creation and at every sunrise. But it is likewise
used to describe the state appearance of Pharaoh—at fes-
tivals, in temples, in the privy council, or at the coronation.
Such a usage proves that it was natural for the Egyptian
to consider these various occurrences as closely similar, as
virtually alike.

For our present purpose we must consider the use of another term in connection with Pharaoh. It is the word
Maat. We have met this word a number of times in the

[27] *Kingship and the Gods* (Chicago, 1948), Ch. 13.

"instructions" for the vizier (page 44) and have translated it there with "justice." But it is a concept belonging
as much to cosmology as to ethics. It is justice as the
divine order of society, but it is also the divine order of
nature as established at the time of creation. In the Pyramid Texts Re is said to have come from the primeval hill,
the place of creation, "after he had put order (Maat) in
the place of chaos." Now the achievement of Pharaoh is
described in exactly the same terms. Tutankhamen records
as follows the acts of his reign, which we know in this
case to have consisted of the restoration of the Amon cult
after the heresy of Akhenaten:

His Majesty drove out disorder (or falsehood) from the Two
Lands so that order (or truth) was again established in its place;
he made disorder (falsehood) an abomination of the land as at
"the first time" (creation).

But we lack words for conceptions which, like Maat, have
ethical as well as metaphysical implications. We must
sometimes translate "order," sometimes "truth," sometimes
"justice"; and the opposite of Maat requires a similar
variety of renderings. In this manner we emphasize un-
wittingly the impossibility of translating Egyptian thoughts
into modern language, for the distinctions which we cannot avoid making did not exist for the Egyptians. Where
society is part of a universal divine order, our contrast has
no meaning. The laws of nature, the laws of society, and
the divine commands all belong to the one category of
what is right. The creator put order (or truth) in the
place of disorder (or falsehood). The creator's successor,
Pharaoh, repeated this significant act at his accession, in
every victory, at the renovation of a temple, and so on.

Amenhotep III stated that he wanted "to make the country flourish as in primeval times by means of the designs of Maat." [28] And nature's course is furthered by the king's acts. We read in the Pyramid Texts:

Heaven is satisfied and the earth rejoices when they hear that King Pepi II has put Maat in the place of falsehood (or disorder).[29]

In the concrete imagery of the Egyptians, the gods are said to live by Maat, which means: The powers immanent in nature function in accordance with the order of creation. Pharaoh stands on a line with the gods in his relation to Maat, as the following quotation shows:

I have made bright the truth (Maat) which he (Re) loves. I know that he lives by it. . . . It is my bread [too]; I too eat of its brightness. I am a likeness from his (Re's) limbs, one with him.[30]

Such texts voice neither presumption nor, when put in the mouths of courtiers, flattery, but sheer theology. And since we have seen that the doctrine of the divinity of Pharaoh found practical expression in the political and social organization of the country, we have no right to doubt that his role as champion of justice was taken seriously. In other words, we must assume that the Egyptian officials found in their function as agents of Pharaoh the same guidance which religious beliefs elsewhere provide. The rebel and the criminal who acted against Pharaoh, be it openly or by faithlessness in Pharaoh's service, headed inevitably for destruction because they moved against the order upon

[28] *Kingship and the Gods,* p. 51.
[29] After K. Sethe, *Die altaegyptischen Pyramidentexte* (Leipzig, 1908–22), § 1775.
[30] After Breasted, *Ancient Records,* II, § 299.

which society, like all that exists, was forever founded. This point of view also explains the fact that the great battle reliefs (Figures 15, 16) always depict the enemies as true representatives of chaos, in notable contrast with the clarity of their royal victor. It likewise explains why the texts always refer to Egypt's enemies in derogatory terms, as wretches or the like. Their annihilation is a foregone conclusion.

Even the pattern to which government in Egypt was made to conform reflects the view of Pharaoh which we have described. The king who lives by Maat, who has a direct knowledge of the predestined order of the universe, cannot consult mere mortals. His decisions are represented as spontaneous creative acts motivated by considerations which are beyond human comprehension, although he may graciously disclose some of them. A session of the privy council is therefore described as follows:

The king made his appearance with the double crown, a sitting took place in the audience-hall. One (that is, the king) took counsel with his suite, the Companions of the Palace (Life! Prosperity! Health!), [and] the officials [of] the place of privacy. One gave commands while they were heard; one took counsel in making them disclosures.[31]

Obviously much had happened before a formal session on this pattern could take place, but the interest for us lies in the form adopted. The verb of the opening sentence, "The king made his appearance with the double crown," is *khay*, which we discussed, and which is also used for the appearance of the sun at dawn. The other point of interest lies in the statement that the king "took counsel in

[31] A. de Buck, in *Analecta orientalia*, XVII (Rome, 1938), 48–57.

making disclosures." His address to the assembled councilors opens appropriately with the following words:

Behold, My Majesty decrees a work and is thinking of a deed,

and after his speech the councilors express merely admiration and consent:

Authoritative utterance is in thy mouth. Understanding follows thee. O Sovereign (Life! Prosperity! Health!), it is thy plans which come to pass.

Nature too responded to the king with acquiescence and support; in other words, the gods acknowledged by their acts that one of them occupied the throne of Egypt. I shall illustrate the Egyptian interpretation of the harmony between society and nature which the king established by the account of a quarrying expedition sent to the Wady Hammamat in the Eleventh Dynasty. It should be remembered that the success of such an undertaking depended very largely upon the initial choice of a site. Since a large body of men was required for the transport of the stones and all supplies had to come up from the Nile Valley, delay might easily lead to a total failure. The worst complication which could occur when a large piece, like a sarcophagus and its lid, had to be quarried, was the discovery of hidden flaws after weeks of work. Hence prospecting for a site took place in that peculiar atmosphere of tension which makes men alive to signs and portents. In the account that follows you will find that the portent, when it occurred, was at once interpreted as a gesture of good will by the "god of the highlands" to Pharaoh; the miracle is said actually to have happened "to the king," although he was several hundred miles away at the time. It is also worth remembering that the inscription was not the official record of the expedition, but especially engraved to commemorate the event it relates. It runs as follows:

This wonder which happened to his majesty: that the beasts of the highlands came down to him; there came a gazelle great with young, going with her face toward the people . . . while her eyes looked backward . . .[32] she did not turn back until she arrived at this august mountain, at this block, it being still in its place, intended for this lid of a sarcophagus. She dropped her young upon it while the army of the king was looking. Then they cut off her neck before it (the block) and brought fire (to offer the gazelle to the god). It (the block) descended in safety (to Egypt).

Now it was the majesty of this august god, the lord of the highlands, who gave [this gift] to his son (King Mentuhotep).[33]

Thus, then, did the people see their state safely integrated with the powers in nature. Those powers, operating beyond the range of man's control, were made to benefit the community through the mediation of the divine king. One might say—though only metaphorically—that the community had sacrificed all freedom in order to acquire this certainty of harmony with the gods.

[32] In other words, while moving away she looked around toward the Egyptians in a way interpreted as an invitation to follow her.
[33] After Breasted, *Ancient Records*, I, § 436.

3

The Egyptian Way of Life

THE "TEACHINGS"

IN discussing the Egyptian way of life we can, for once, dispense with inferences. The Egyptians were quite explicit on the subject. They cherished books expounding the good life and the way of achieving it. Some of these works date from the third millennium B.C. and were still being copied after more than a thousand years. Others were composed in later times. It would seem that we have here material for a history of ideas, and modern scholars have sometimes used these texts to describe a development of social and ethical thought in Egypt. I do not think that such an interpretation is tenable if we study the evidence without prejudice—that is, without an evolutionary bias. The differences between the earlier and the later texts seem largely to have been caused by accidents of preservation, while their resemblance consists, on the contrary, in a significant uniformity of tenor. Moreover, the differences were not considered important by the Egyptians themselves. Continually copying very ancient teachings, they showed that, in their opinion, these had lost nothing of their validity with the lapse of time. In this as in other respects Egyptian culture preserved its distinctive character throughout its long history, and we may, therefore, speak of an Egyptian way of life without dwelling on the modifications which the basic conception underwent in the course of time.

The great popularity of the "teachings" is in itself revealing. The Egyptians were evidently convinced that the good
life could be taught. Such a conviction betrays a surpris-
ing confidence in the efficacy of man's understanding; it
reflects a feeling of security, of being in a world which is
neither hostile nor, in the last analysis, problematical. This
feeling was peculiar to the Egyptians. In Mesopotamia,
for instance, the prevailing mood was one of uncertainty:
the gods "determined destiny" year by year and were
guided by considerations incomprehensible to man. The
keynote of the Hebrew prophets was deep anxiety: they
knew the divine commands but they also knew that man's
laxity was incorrigible and God's wrath unallayed. And so
it may be due to the serenity of the Egyptian "teachings"
that they are viewed so rarely in this religious context
where they belong. They are usually interpreted as secular
guides of conduct; but the contrast between the secular
and the religious is difficult to draw in ancient culture and,
in any case, the current treatment of the "teachings" ob-
scures their true significance and their peculiarly Egyptian
character.

The authors of the "teachings" do not present themselves as priests or even as prophets. They appear as aged
officials at the end of active and successful careers, desirous
to let their children profit by their experience. The "Teachings of Kagemni"—reputedly a vizier of the Sixth Dynasty
—end as follows:

The vizier had his children called after he had completed [his
treatise on] the ways of mankind and on their character as encountered by him. And he said unto them: "All that is in this
book, hear it as if (?) I spake it. . . ." They read it as it stood in
writing, and it was better in their heart than everything that was

in this entire land; they stood and they sat in accordance there-with.[1]

The last sentence means, of course, that they modeled their whole lives on these instructions. But occasionally one feels a malicious desire to take the words literally, for the "teachings" seem to us at times to descend to entirely trivial matters; this happens without any transition, sometimes immediately after truly momentous questions have been raised. Such an inconsequential arrangement character-izes many books of ancient "wisdom"; the books of Proverbs and Ecclesiastes are cases in point. The absence of a sys-tematic arrangement is due to the traditional character of the contents. There is no need of a closely knit argument; striking images, incisive wording are all that is required to give a fresh appeal to the truth of familiar viewpoints. But how are we to account for the fact that the "Teachings of Ptahhotep" contain, among other things which we should not consider important, the following advice to a man in-vited to dine with his superiors (I paraphrase): Take the food that is served to you; don't stare at the great man's plate but look down on your own; talk only when spoken to; laugh when he laughs, he will like that; you will be agreeable to him, and that is just as well for you, for you never know what a magnate may be up to next.

This kind of advice seems so thoroughly transparent that we smile at Ptahhotep's "wisdom." But we risk miss-ing the overtones of this ancient voice if we are so easily satisfied that we have understood it. We need to listen with greater attention.

[1] Adolf Erman, *The Literature of the Ancient Egyptians*, tr. A. M. Black-man (London, 1927), p. 67.

THE PRAGMATIC MISINTERPRETATION

Let us take a pronouncement which precedes the one I paraphrased:

If thou art a leader who directs the affairs of a multitude, strive after every excellence until there be no fault in thy nature. Maat is good and its worth is lasting. It has not been disturbed since the day of its creator, whereas he who transgresses its ordinances is punished. It lies as a path in front even of him who knows nothing. Wrongdoing (?) has never yet brought its venture to port. It is true that evil may gain wealth but the strength of truth is that it lasts; a man can say: "It was the property of my father." [2]

This "teaching," like the preceding one, possesses an obvious meaning. It simply states that honesty is the best policy. A high official must strive after every excellence; that implies that he must be true and just, for whoever acts against Maat comes ultimately to grief. It is true that ill-gotten wealth exists, but it rests on an insecure foundation. On the other hand, whatever one possesses by right gives the satisfaction of safety. This obvious, superficial meaning of the text is emphasized in the most recent translation which renders part of it as follows: "Justice (Maat) is of advantage and its utility lasts." Here, indeed, is pragmatism pure and simple, but it does not render, I think, the Egyptian point of view.

The conception of Maat integrates the "teaching" of our quotation. And when we read that "Maat has not been disturbed since the day of its creator" we find, in the middle of a quasi-practical piece of advice, the fundamental

[2] After Erman, *Literature*, p. 57, and J. A. Wilson, in *The Intellectual Adventure of Ancient Man* (Chicago, 1946), pp. 99–100.

doctrine of Egyptian religion. We discussed the conception
of Maat, with its unmodern, untranslatable combination of
meanings, in the preceding chapter. The Egyptians recognized a divine order, established at the time of creation;
this order is manifest in nature in the normalcy of phenomena; it is manifest in society as justice; and it is manifest in an individual's life as truth. Maat *is* this order, the
essence of existence, whether we recognize it or not. Hence
Ptahhotep's remark: "It is as a path even in front of him
who knows nothing." Hence also the sequence, without
any transition, of his two statements that an official must
"strive after excellence," and that "Maat is good and its
worth is lasting." The excellence of the official consisted in
his agreement with Maat—justice, truth. The statement
about Maat, in the version we use, is a little colorless:
"Maat is good and its worth is lasting." But if we render
"Maat is of advantage and its utility lasts," we convey an
opportunism which the original does not possess, and
which violates the spirit of the ancients. The word *akh,*
which is translated "to be good" or "to be of advantage,"
possesses, according to the dictionary, an *"unklare ver-
schwommene Bedeutung."* But this impression of an obscure and fluid meaning is often caused, not by any lack of
clarity in the original, but by the incompatibility of ancient
and modern conceptions. Such a discrepancy exists in the
case of Maat, a concept which is totally alien to contemporary thought and which therefore cannot be matched
by any modern term. We should have to render it, at one
and the same time, as a social, an ethical, and a cosmological conception. *Akh* seems to be untranslatable for
similar reasons; it may mean "to be agreeable," "to be ad-
vantageous," but also "to be effective, splendid, sacred,

transfigured"—meanings which find their common root in the concept of harmony with the divine order of the universe. I should like philologists to investigate whether this basic conception does not tinge, however faintly, all uses of the word; the pragmatism of Ptahhotep would then appear once more to possess a religious background which differentiates it *toto caelo* from the pragmatism of our day. Ptahhotep's statement: "Maat has not been disturbed since the day of its creator," induced Breasted, in 1912, to speak of "the complaisant optimism which characterizes his maxims." [3] We now realize that it indicates no such thing, but represents, on the contrary, the deep religious conviction which inspired the "teachings."

The conception of Maat expresses the Egyptian belief that the universe is changeless and that all apparent opposites must, therefore, hold each other in equilibrium. Such a belief has definite consequences in the field of moral philosophy. It puts a premium on whatever exists with a semblance of permanence. It excludes ideals of progress, utopias of any kind, revolutions, or any other radical changes in existing conditions. It allows a man "to strive after every excellence until there be no fault in his nature," but that implies, as we have seen, harmony with the established order, the latter not taken in any vague and general way but quite specifically as that which exists with seeming permanence. In this way the belief in a static universe enhances, for instance, the significance of established authority; hence correct behavior towards one's superiors possessed for the Egyptians a significance which we may circumscribe, but which we cannot com-

[3] J. H. Breasted, *Development of Religion and Thought in Ancient Egypt* (New York, 1912), p. 142.

prehend. In the same way inherited possessions owned a sanctity which no merely acquired wealth could ever obtain.

But when a predestined order is recognized in so many quasi-permanent features of society, when actuality, in so far as it is traditional, receives a moral sanction, all rules of conduct become practical rules. There can be no contrast between *savoir-faire*—worldly wisdom—and ethical behavior. Conceptions which we distinguish as contrasts thus turn out to be identical for the Egyptian; statements of his, which have for us a pragmatic ring, appear to be transfused with religious reverence.

SUCCESS AS ATTUNEMENT

The Egyptian did not believe the good life easy of attainment. It is true that it could—and should—be taught, for, as Ptahhotep has it: "There is no child that of itself has understanding." And King Merikare was given the following instruction by his father:

Copy thy fathers who have gone before thee. . . . Behold, their words are recorded in writing. Open and read and copy him who knows(?). Thus he who is skilled becomes one who is instructed.[4]

But it was not only ignorance that threatened to lead man astray. His passionate nature presented as great a danger. The Egyptian was well acquainted with the whole range of the seven deadly sins. Hence the "teachings" distinguish two temperaments: the "passionate man" and the self-disciplined, the so-called "silent man." The passionate man is garrulous, quarrelsome, grasping, arbitrary,

[4] Alan H. Gardiner, in *Journal of Egyptian Archaeology,* I (1914), 25.

overweening. The silent man is patient, modest, calm, up to a point self-effacing, but above all master of himself under all circumstances.

The destinies of these two temperaments are contrasted as follows by Amenemope:

> As for the passionate man in the temple, he is like a tree growing in the open. Suddenly [comes] its loss of foliage, and its end is reached in the shipyards; [or] it is floated far from its place, and a flame is its burial shroud.
>
> [But] the truly silent man holds himself apart. He is like a tree growing in a garden. It flourishes; it doubles its fruit; it [stands] before its lord. Its fruit is sweet; its shade is pleasant; and its end is reached in the garden.[5]

We are apt to misunderstand the ideal of the silent man. It does not exalt submissiveness, meekness, or any kind of otherworldliness. The silent man is pre-eminently the successful man. High officials describe themselves as "truly silent," [6] and they do so not with a Christian estimate of the spirit of humility, but with a wisdom which is peculiarly Egyptian. They consider that the go-getter jeopardizes his success by the violence of his passion; he destroys that harmonious integration in the existing order which alone is effective. True wisdom is true power; but it means mastery over one's impulses, and silence is a sign not of humility, but of superiority. One must be able to avoid getting involved in situations in which one is likely to be carried away by one's feelings. Hence Amenemope counsels:

> and give way unto him that attacketh.
> Pause before an intruder,

[5] After Wilson, in *The Intellectual Adventure of Ancient Man,* pp. 114–15.
[6] *Ibid.,* p. 114.

> Sleep a night before speaking;
>> the storm, it bursts forth like flame in straw.
>
> The passionate man in his hour
>> withdraw thyself before him;
> Leave him to his own devices;
>> God will know how to reply to him.[7]

The use of the word "God," which is common in the "teachings," requires comment. The original uses *netjer*, which may mean "a god," "the god," or "God." "A god" is too vague and "the god" too definite; the exact meaning is "the god with whom you have to reckon in the circumstances." Egyptologists generally translate it "God," and that rightly, since the relation of the Egyptian to the god with whom he had to reckon at a given moment was, temporarily, almost exclusive of all others. The teaching of Amenemope indicates that the passionate man "in his hour" —that is, when he is carried away—will certainly come up against the god who is concerned with the particular situation in which the conflict takes place. But one must master the storm that bursts forth like a fire in straw when one is provoked by an intruder or an attacker; it is this storm in his own heart which the wise man suppresses.

Now if one should decline to be drawn into a position where deliberation is impossible, it is all the more necessary that one should avoid creating such a situation:

> Say not: find me a strong chief,
>> for a man in thy city has injured me; . . .
> Really, thou knowest not the designs of God,
>> thou canst not realize (?) the morrow.
>
> Put thyself in the hands of God
>> and thy tranquillity shall overthrow them (the enemies).

[7] F. Ll. Griffith, in *Journal of Egyptian Archaeology*, XII (1926), 201.

> In fact, the crocodile which gives no sound,
> of him above all fear is inveterate.[8]

Notice that the advice to trust in God is tempered with the reminder that the man who is master of his emotions is truly redoubtable: "Thy tranquillity shall overthrow them." The point is emphasized by the image of the dreaded voiceless crocodile. There is no question of declining to quarrel out of meekness or love for one's fellow men. One avoids a conflict because it would be unwise to get involved in a situation which may imply more complications than one can foresee ("thou knowest not the designs of God"), and where deliberate and effective action may become impossible.

Restraint of passions and an avoidance of extremes in general, characterize the wise man. One must neither be carried away by one's anxieties nor waste one's chances by carelessness. One must keep to the middle way in everything. Ptahhotep said:

He who reckons all day has never a happy moment;
He who feasts all day cannot keep his family.
One reaches one's goal according to one's steering
While [in turn] one steering oar is released and the other grasped.
He who listens to his heart [alone] will come to: Had I but . . . !

in other words, to fruitless regrets.[9]

To the dangers of ignorance and lack of control over one's passions must be added that of pride. One risks being arrogant because of one's spiritual gifts, or because

---

[8] After A. de Buck, in *Nieuw theologisch Tydschrift*, XXI (Haarlem, 1932), 339.
[9] *Ibid.*, p. 347.

one ascribes to one's own effectiveness things which are really no more than good fortune, which means, a gift of the gods. Ptahhotep warns against both forms of pride:

Be not arrogant because of thy knowledge, and have no confidence in that thou art a learned man. Take counsel with the ignorant as with the wise, for the limits of artistry cannot be reached and no artist fully possesses his skill. A good discourse is more hidden than the precious green stone, yet it is found with slave girls over the millstones.[10]

And so also with material success:

If thou ploughest and there is growth in the field, God causes it to be much in thy hand. Do not boast about this among thy kindred. Great is the respect that the silent one calls forth.[11]

The last two sentences are very revealing. The Egyptian judged pride more like the Greeks than like the Hebrews. It was not a sin of the creature against his maker but a loss of the sense of proportion, a self-reliance, a self-assertion which passed the bounds of man and hence led to disaster. But while the Greek *hubris* was overtaken by Nemesis, the gods' resentment, the Egyptian's pride dislocated him within his appropriate setting, society. Ptahhotep states that he who exceeds his bounds by claiming credit for what is really a gift of the gods loses the place which an effective, self-possessed, wise man occupies: "Do not boast . . . among thy kindred for great is the respect that the silent one calls forth." The conceited man earns scorn, and thus a subtle shift in his relationships destroys his status in the community. Note that Ptahhotep, like Amenemope who lived perhaps two thousand years later, represents silence

[10] After Erman, *Literature*, p. 56.
[11] After A. de Buck, in *Nieuw theologisch Tydschrift*, p. 341.

not as a quality of the timid, the humble, or the meek, but of the superior man, whose mastery over himself constitutes an achievement acknowledged by all.[12]

The Egyptians declared the punishment of pride and other failings to be the business of the gods, but they believed that divine retribution often acted not through a direct interference in human affairs, but indirectly, through the maintenance of Maat, the established order. From this point of view a man's success in life appears as proof of his frictionless integration with that order. The successful man possesses a remarkable quality and disposes of an impersonal force because of his harmonious attunement to society and nature. Hence those who are less fortunate should attempt to profit and improve their situation by a close association with such a man. This is the meaning of the following "teaching" of Ptahhotep:

If thou art wretched, then thou shouldst serve a man of repute, so that thy conduct be good before God; and it should be one of whom thou knowest that he was formerly insignificant. Do not raise up thine heart against him (i.e., don't be proud) on account of that which thou knowest about him from the past, but honor him on account of that which fell to his lot. For wealth does not come of itself, but it is their (the gods') ordinance for him whom they love. . . . It is God who creates his success and he protects him even when he sleeps.[13]

The unfortunate man is here advised to cling to one who

[12] The insistence, in the instruction of the vizier (p. 44), on the fear which he must inspire is therefore perfectly in keeping with the ideal of the "silent man" which the same instructions, by implication, set before him. Notice (p. 46 and pp. 149 ff.) how the High Steward Rensi, in the tale of the Eloquent Peasant, behaves as a "silent man" by appearing unmoved until the time has come to reward the peasant and to destroy Thothnakht.

[13] After A. de Buck, in *Nieuw theologisch Tydschrift,* p. 342.

has been conspicuously successful, as if the strong current of the latter's life would allow the wretch to get afloat again, and would even carry him out of the backwater where his maladaptation has grounded him. Conversely, it is most unwise to associate with a misfit; this is the true meaning of the repeated warnings against bad company which are found in the "teachings" and which we are very likely to misconstrue. Kagemni counsels:

If thou sittest with a greedy person, eat thou only when his meal is over, and if thou sittest with a drunkard, take thou only when his desire is satisfied.[14]

The usual comment on this type of advice is totally inadequate. It is neither a rule of good conduct, nor a plan for making a man popular and likely to gain advancement— in fact, I can think of no behavior more likely to get one into trouble. Kagemni evidently wants his young man to dissociate himself in a conspicuous way from those who are acting against Maat and who are therefore bound to come to grief sooner or later. This was a matter of serious concern, a truly religious preoccupation, as is shown by the fact that one is advised to sever the bonds even with one's own son if he proves hopelessly corrupt. We must remember how much a son meant to the ancient Egyptians to gauge the full weight of the following words of Ptahhotep:

(If, after warning and correction, thy son continues to do wrong)
    then drive him away . . . he is not thy son, he is not born to
    thee. . . .
Reject him as one whom they (the gods) have condemned;
He is one who is damned already in the flesh.

14 Erman, *Literature*, p. 66.

He whom they guide does not go astray,
But he whom they leave without a boat cannot make the crossing.[15]

But if success is proof of harmony with the gods, it also
imposes upon the man who is "right" the obligation of
increasing the well-being of society by assisting those who
are less fortunate:

> A man whom his god has built up should foster many.[16]

So also Amenemope:

> If thou find a large debt against a poor man,
>   make it into three parts;
> forgive two, let one remain;
>   thou wilt find it a path of life;
> thou wilt lie down at night and sleep soundly.
>   On the morrow thou wilt find it like good news.[17]

This profound experience of lasting satisfaction after a gen-
erous act was not caused by the awareness of having obeyed
a divine commandment; it was a direct consequence of being in harmony with Maat. Righteousness produces joy, evil
brings misfortune—but this phrase possessed more pro-
fundity in Egypt than it has in modern pragmatism. For
our word "righteous" renders most imperfectly the Egyptian qualification of an action which we should call so, but
which, to the Egyptians, passed beyond the scope of ethics
and affected the very existence of man and of society in
nature.

[15] After Erman, *Literature,* p. 59, and A. de Buck, in *Nieuw theologisch
Tydschrift,* p. 342.
[16] Gardiner, ed., *Hieratic Papyri in the British Museum,* Third Series:
Chester Beatty Gift (London, 1935), Papyrus No. IV.
[17] Griffith, in *Journal of Egyptian Archaeology,* XII (1926), 213.

THE ABSENCE OF THE CONCEPT OF SIN

We have so far mainly considered the positive and didactic statements about the good life; we have seen that it was endangered by ignorance, passion, and pride. But the question remains whether the Egyptians, conceiving *goodness* in the sense we have described, showed any preoccupation with the concept of evil. The answer is that they did so only to a very limited extent. We have seen in earlier chapters that they believed the universe to contain opposing forces in perennial equilibrium. Evil, then, had its appointed place, counterbalanced—and kept in place—by good. The difference from biblical religion is most striking in this respect. There are many Egyptian words denoting evil acts, but I doubt whether any should be rendered by "sin," if one grants that word its proper theological connotation. The Egyptian viewed his misdeeds not as sins, but as aberrations. They would bring him unhappiness because they disturbed his harmonious integration with the existing world; they might even be explicitly disapproved by one or another of the gods, but these were always ready to welcome his better insight:

> Though the servant was disposed to do evil,
> Yet is the Lord disposed to be merciful.
> The Lord of Thebes (Amon) passes not a whole day wroth:
> His wrath is finished in a moment, and nought is left.[18]

It is especially significant that the Egyptians never showed any trace of feeling unworthy of the divine mercy. For he who errs is not a sinner but a fool, and his conversion to a better way of life does not require repentance but a better understanding. When Amenemope states:

[18] Battiscombe Gunn, in *Journal of Egyptian Archaeology*, III (1916), 85.

God is in his perfection, man is in his inadequacy,[19]

the contrast is a simple statement of fact which entirely lacks the deeply disturbing overtones which it would possess in a biblical context. It merely expresses an existing situation and warns man against overconfidence. In the Egyptians' universe man had his place, and that admittedly below the gods. The command of the Old Testament that man should be "holy" (for example, Exodus 19:6) or the terrifying exhortation of Matthew 5:48: "Be ye therefore perfect, even as your Father which is in heaven is perfect"—would have seemed to the ancient Egyptian a mere confusion of the issue.

Lack of insight or lack of self-restraint were at the root of man's misfortunes, but not a basic corruption. And yet the Egyptian knew that not all men desired to follow the path of measured harmony which led to happiness. They admitted, therefore, something resembling divine grace; or rather, in the way of the Greeks, they stressed its opposite by stating that the gods blind him whom they wish to destroy. In Egypt the doomed man is deaf to the teachings of the sages; he becomes, in Ptahhotep's words, "one that hears not":

He whom God loves, hears, but he whom God hates, hears not. It is the heart that makes the owner into one that hears or one that hears not. His heart is a man's fortune. . . . As for a fool that hears not, he can do nothing at all. He regards knowledge as ignorance and good as bad. He lives on that of which one dies; his food is untruth.[20]

Untruth, falsehood, disorder, the opposite of Maat, is that

---

[19] After Griffith, in *Journal of Egyptian Archaeology*, XII (1926), 216.
[20] After Erman, *Literature*, p. 64, and A. de Buck, in *Nieuw theologisch Tydschrift*, p. 337.

of which one dies. It makes life impossible. How this is to be understood is shown by Amenemope:

> Speak not to a man in falsehood,
>   the abomination of God;
> sever not thy heart from thy tongue,
>   that all thy ways may be successful.

We shall no longer interpret this "teaching" as a shallow piece of opportunism, of the type, "It pays to be honest." Ptahhotep's remark that falsehood is that "of which one dies" indicates the argument underlying Amenemope's statement. Falsehood is the opposite of Maat; it is chaos, "the abomination of God," that which is perennially defeated in the order of the universe. Hence it is fatal for a man to identify himself with it. Yet he does so when he is dishonest, when he "severs his heart from his tongue"; consequently he cannot be *effective* when he does so; that is the meaning of the word "successful" in our quotation, as is proved by the concrete example with which Amenemope continues his "teaching." Do not simulate friendship towards your enemy:

> Say not to him "Hail to thee" in falsehood
> When there is terror in thy belly,

for one cannot bring that off. On the other hand, do not dissimulate your conviction even when others disagree, but act, again, all of a piece:

> Be thou resolute before other people,
>   for one is safe at the hand of God;
> hated of God is the falsifier of words,
>   his great abomination is the dissembler . . .[21]

[21] This and the preceding quotations are from Griffith, in *Journal of Egyptian Archaeology*, XII (1926), 209–10.

Such words have a familiar ring but they really represent a totally alien point of view. God's hatred of the dissembler is not an ethical, but a cosmic force. It destroys the dishonest man, not because he acts against a divine commandment, but because he is not in harmony with Maat, the universal order. One might object that the Egyptian expressed the conflict as one which involves a personal god, not an impersonal force. That is true, and the notion of an impersonal force is in any case modern, not ancient.[22] I have therefore avoided saying that he who moves against Maat is destroyed automatically. But is it not remarkable that none of the gods are mentioned by name in any of the "teachings"? When the Egyptians appeal to "God," namely, to "the god with whom you have to reckon in the circumstances," they impart to the divine interest in man's behavior a distinctly impersonal character. The whole pantheon, every one of the gods, required the "right" conduct. An individual might feel more closely connected with one deity than with another, but the personal character of such a relationship was created by the worshiper, not—as in the Bible—by the deity.

We have a number of texts in which the loyalty of devotees of particular gods found expression. They are hymns in which ordinary people pray or render thanks for a favorable turn in their fortunes. The gods to whom gratitude is expressed differ, but the spirit and sometimes even the wording remains the same throughout these texts. This can be understood if we remember that the Egyptian gods were imperfectly individualized because they were immanent in nature (pages 25–29). They differed in their

[22] See *The Intellectual Adventure of Ancient Man*, pp. 15 ff.

spheres of action, but hardly in their characters. And thus
man stood in the same relation to all of them, even though a
scribe might feel special allegiance to Thoth, an artist to
Ptah, a craftsman in the necropolis to Hathor, or to the
Goddess of the West, or to the Peak, the splendid mountain over the cemeteries in which this goddess was immanent. But such differences are inessential; all the gods
functioned within the established order; they all "lived by
Maat" and consequently they all hated "untruth." We may
say that in Egyptian thought Maat, the divine order, mediated between man and the gods. On the whole, when man
erred, he did not commit, in the first place, a crime against
a god; he moved against the established order, and one
god or another saw to it that that order was vindicated.
We do not find in Egypt the violent conflict which is characteristic of biblical religion. Man is not seen in rebellion
against the command of God nor does he experience the
intensity and range of feelings from contrition to grace
which characterize the main personages of the Old and
New Testaments. By the same token the theme of God's
wrath is practically unknown in Egyptian literature; for the
Egyptian, in his aberrations, is not a sinner whom God re-
jects but an ignorant man who is disciplined and corrected.
This is well illustrated by the following hymn, written by
a worker in the Theban necropolis after he had been cured
of an illness:

> I was an ignorant man and foolish,
> Who knew neither good nor evil.
> I wrought the transgression against the Peak,
> And she chastised me.
> I was in her hand by night as by day

> "Mark," I will say to great and little
> That are among the workmen:
> "Be ye ware of the Peak!
> For that a lion is within the Peak.
> She smites with the smiting of a savage lion.
> She pursues him that transgresses against her."
>
> I called upon my Mistress;
> I found that she came to me with sweet airs;
> She was merciful to me,
> (After) she had made me behold her hand.
> She turned again to me in mercy:
> She caused me to forget the sickness that had
>   been [upon] me.[23]

But another addresses the sun-god:

> Thou Sole and Only One, Harakhte,
> Like whom there is here no other!
> Who protects millions
> And delivers hundreds of thousands!
> The Savior of him that cries unto him,
> The Lord of Heliopolis!
> Punish me not for my many misdeeds.
> I am one that knows not himself (?).
> I am a witless man.
> All day long I follow my mouth like an ox after fodder.[24]

Yet another man invokes Amon:

> Thou art [Amon], the Lord of him that is silent;
> Who comest at the voice of the humble man.
> I call upon thee when I am in distress:
> And thou comest that thou mayest save me;
> That thou mayest give breath to him that is wretched;
> That thou mayest save me that am in bondage.[25]

[23] After Gunn, in *Journal of Egyptian Archaeology*, III (1916), 86–87.
[24] After Erman, *Literature*, p. 307.
[25] Gunn, in *Journal of Egyptian Archaeology*, III (1916), 84.

The difference between these texts lies not in the picture they give of the different gods, but in that which the devotee gives of himself. And there we meet the same viewpoint as in the "teachings," although the latter were intended for the educated public and the hymns belong to the sphere of popular literature. In these hymns, the men describe their faults as the consequence of ignorance; when they approve of themselves they claim to be like "the silent man." And the texts derive no distinctive features at all from the character of the particular god to whom they happen to be addressed.

There are a few exceptional documents among these popular hymns. For the need of divine sanction and support for a line of conduct which, although it was known to be right, was nevertheless difficult to adhere to, that need was sometimes so great that it could not be satisfied by the very generalized connection between the Egyptian gods and the moral code. In some cases, therefore, the gods were given attributes which have only an emotional, not a theological, justification. The following hymn, addressed to Thoth, allows us to demonstrate this peculiar elaboration of the ordinary themes with great clarity. Thoth, the god of scribes, was manifest in the moon and was represented as an ibis or as a baboon (page 10 and Figures 3, 4, 5). He was entirely unconnected with vegetation or with the power in water. Yet images derived from these spheres of natural life play a predominant part in the poem which a scribe addressed to the god of his profession. It starts by emphasizing the guardianship of Thoth over scribes:

O Thoth, take me to Hermopolis, to thy city, where it is pleasant to live.

Thou suppliest what I need in bread and beer and thou keepest
watch over my mouth when I speak.

Would that I had Thoth behind me tomorrow (when I shall
die)!
Come to me when I enter before the Lords of Maat (the judges
in the hereafter)
And so shall I come forth justified.
Thou great dom palm, sixty cubits high, whereon are fruits;
Stones are in the fruits and water is in the stones.
Thou who bringest water to a distant place, come deliver me, the
silent man.
Thoth, thou sweet well for one who thirsts in the desert;
It is closed for one who argues but open for him who keeps
silence.
The silent one comes and finds the well.
The hot-headed comes and thou art [choked?].[26]

The last verse shows that the elaborate imagery of the
poem serves to bring the opposition of the passionate and
the silent man in relation with the god to whom the scribe
is particularly attached. His feelings evoke images of the
greatest delights, the shade of the palm and the cool water
from the well. Hence the associative progression of the
images: the dom palm of great height; the fruit; the
moisture-filled kernels in the fruit; the moisture that re-
freshes the thirsting; the well from which the "right," the
"silent" man draws strength and consolation.

THE SIGNIFICANCE OF TRADITION

The usual and less original texts merely express the dependence of man upon the gods; similarly the "teachings"
of Amenemope express this thought as follows:

> Verily, man is clay and straw,
> God is his fashioner;

[26] After Erman, *Literature*, pp. 305 f.

He pulls down and builds up each day;
He makes a thousand dependents at his will
Or he makes a thousand men into overseers(?).[27]

The significant and (to us) extraordinary fact is this, however: While in the Old and New Testaments man's dependence upon God finds a correlate in God's concern for man, the Egyptian gods remain aloof. Their relationship to man is indirect. This is true whether we consider the Egyptians as members of society or as individuals. The actions of the community were guided by the divine king with whom alone the other gods communicated. The actions of individuals lacked divine guidance altogether, as far as we know. The gods were known to require, in a general way, that man respect Maat. But in this they did hardly more than endorse a necessary condition of existence. There were no specific divine commands which gave man directives for the shaping of his actions. We have seen that it was "right" to enjoy an inheritance, to respect established authority, to maintain the unity of "heart and tongue," conviction and speech. But nowhere do we find the gods specifically commanding: "Thou shalt do these things"; we do not even find that a rule of conduct or a set of "teachings" is recommended as inspired or approved by a god. The gods were immanent in the phenomena and therefore remained impersonal. And so the Egyptians present us with one more paradox: living under the rule of a god incarnate, they were dependent on human wisdom alone for direction in their way of life. Here lies the importance of the "teachings" which we have quoted. The mature reflection of the sages, the experience accumulated through generations, supplied the guidance of which men stood in need.

[27] After Griffith, in *Journal of Egyptian Archaeology*, XII (1926), 221.

The wisdom of the "teachings" was rooted, of course, in the less articulate convictions of the people; the sayings clarified an accepted point of view and illustrated, by telling similes and examples, what actions and what attitudes were in harmony with the created order, were "right" in the different situations which could arise in a man's life. That the "teachings" were considered as a thoroughly worked-through version of common wisdom is said in the "Instructions for King Merikare": "Truth comes to him fully kneaded like the sayings of the ancestors." [28] The "teachings" are, moreover, not the only texts describing the Egyptians' view of what constitutes the right way of life, and the nondidactic inscriptions have the same tenor as the "teachings." For instance, the ideal biographies which we find in a number of tombs refer in the same general way to the divine sanction of the accepted way of life. A high official of the Old Kingdom, Pepinakht, describes himself as follows:

I was one who said that which was good, and repeated that which was loved. Never did I say anything evil to a powerful one against any people, [for] I desired that it be well with me in the great god's presence.[29] I gave bread to the hungry, and clothing to the naked. Never did I judge two brothers in such a way that a son was deprived of his paternal possession. I was one beloved of his father, praised of his mother, whom his brothers and sisters loved.[30]

Here we meet again the appreciation of charity in word and deed, and of the sanctity of inheritance which we

[28] Gardiner, in *Journal of Egyptian Archaeology*, I (1914), 25; Erman, *Literature*, p. 76.
[29] The "great god" is probably the king; if so, Pepinakht's text shows once more that the Egyptian ideal of kingship was effective. The desire to stand well with Pharaoh inspired the official to behave well.
[30] Breasted, *Ancient Records*, I, § 357.

have already come to understand (pages 62–65) as a consequence of the Egyptians' valuation of permanence in all
conditions.

Poets living a thousand years after Pepinakht reflect the
same ideals and the same feeling that the right life receives an impersonal and indirect sanction from the gods.
As an example I shall quote a text which is neither didactic
nor biographical, namely, one of the harpers' songs recently
studied and translated by Dr. Miriam Lichtheim.[31] It
combines an encouragement to enjoy life with a description
of the man who lives rightly and is therefore predisposed
to be happy. The song ends as follows:

> Make holiday, verily, verily!
> Put incense and fine oil together beside thee
> And garlands of lotus and rrmt-flowers upon thy breast.
> The woman whom thou lovest,
> It is she who sits at thy side.
> Thou shouldst not anger thy heart
> Over anything that has happened.
> Put music before thee,
> Do not recall evil, abomination of the god;
> Bethink thee of joys,
> Thou righteous, thou just and true man,
> Calm, friendly, content, relaxed,
> Happy, not speaking evil.
> Give drunkenness to thy heart every day
> Until the day comes in which there is landing!

The ideal described in the last five lines of this song is
identical with that which the "teachings" delineate.

We may now summarize: The Egyptian way of life,
signposted by the wisdom of the sages, appears as one not
of struggle but of harmony. Within the all-inclusive unity

[31] *Journal of Near Eastern Studies*, IV (1945), 201.

of nature and society man could move with dignity, safety, and happiness. But you will have noticed at the end of the harper's song that a limit was set to joy: "Until the day comes in which there is landing." The reference is to the landing of the funeral barge at the west bank of the Nile when the dead man is carried to his tomb. We shall discuss in the next chapter the attitude of the Egyptians towards death. Our quotation shows that they were prepared to remember its inevitability even while in a festive mood; in fact, they were deeply preoccupied with the thought of death and during their lifetimes spent much of their substance on the equipment of their tombs.

Here it remains for us to consider the attitude of the Egyptians under circumstances which made the validity of their way of life seem problematical. This happened when political catastrophe overtook them and the established order, which they regarded as rooted in the order of creation, was destroyed. Egypt's isolated position behind desert barriers protected it against foreign interference and thus the safety of the state was but rarely endangered. But towards the end of the third millennium B.C. the central government weakened and disintegrated; local magnates usurped the power which was the prerogative of Pharaoh; and Asiatics entered the land. This period of disaster, following the first great realization of Egyptian statehood in the Pyramid age, made a terrible impression upon thinking men. The literary works in which their thoughts were expressed show a significant emphasis: the presence of the Asiatics, however hurtful to their pride, was much less subject to complaint than the demoralization and confusion of the country. This was the truly intolerable feature of the times which left men shocked and bewildered. For when an established order possesses moral sanction, its overthrow leaves man without certainty or direction. The texts, indeed, pile image upon image to make it clear that the world is upside down:

Nay, but gold and lapis lazuli, silver and turquoise . . . are hung about the necks of slave-girls. But noble ladies walk through the land, and mistresses of houses say: "Would that we had something we might eat." [32]

Nay, but the citizens have been placed over the mill-stones. They that were clad in fine linen are beaten

. . .

Nay, but the children of princes, men dash them against walls. The children that have been earnestly desired, they are exposed upon the desert. Khnum (the god who models man before birth) complaineth because of his (useless exertions).[33]

One might like to interpret these texts as expressions of regret by the privileged classes that common people now assert equal rights. But the texts are quite explicit in describing the general nature of the catastrophe. Succinctly:

The country turns round like a potter's wheel.[34]

As to the poor:

Nay, but the roads . . . are watched. Men sit in the bushes until the benighted traveller comes so that they may rob him of his load. What is upon him is stolen. He getteth blows of the stick to smell and is slain wrongfully

. . .

Nay, but men feed on herbs and drink water. No fruit nor herbs are longer found for the birds, and the offal is robbed from the mouth of the swine. . . .[35]

[32] After Erman, *Literature*, p. 96.   [33] *Ibid.*, p. 98.   [34] *Ibid.*, p. 95.
[35] *Ibid.*, p. 99.

In a text which assumes the form of prophecy we read:

Men shall fashion arrows of copper, that they may beg for bread with blood. Men laugh with a laughter of disease.[36]

As a result of these conditions:

> Great and small say: "I wish I were dead!" [37]

Some thoughtful men have described not merely the prevailing anarchy, but their own reaction to it:

I am meditating upon what has happened, on the things that have come to pass throughout the land. Changes take place; it is not like last year, and one year is more burdensome than the other. The land is in confusion. . . . Maat is cast out and iniquity [sits] in the council chamber. The plans of the gods are destroyed and their ordinances transgressed. The land is in misery, mourning is in every place, towns and villages lament.[38]

In these words we find confirmed what we might have expected on the basis of the "teachings": a collapse of the established order would leave the Egyptian totally disorientated. And so we may understand a most remarkable composition written in these disturbed times and known to us as the "Dialogue of a Man Weary of Life with His Soul." We shall discuss this later (page 142 and following) but must here comment on its general trend. The man who speaks has the intention of committing suicide, but he does not state that he has personally suffered injustice. His complaints concern the destruction of the social order in which life has value:

> To whom can I speak today?
> The gentle man has perished,
> The violent man has access to everybody. . . .

[36] *Ibid.*, p. 114.   [37] *Ibid.*, p. 97.   [38] *Ibid.*, p. 109.

> To whom can I speak today?
> The iniquity that smites the land
> It has no end.[39]

In contrast with this aspect of society death offers release:

> Death stands before me today
> As a man longs to see his house
> After he has spent many years in captivity.

When the established order from which the Egyptian way of life derived its orientation was destroyed, life became meaningless and, therefore, unbearable.

[39] Wilson, in *The Intellectual Adventure of Ancient Man,* pp. 102–3.

4

The Egyptian Hope

THE PREOCCUPATION WITH DEATH

ONE theme has recurred time and again in these chapters: the peculiar attitude of the Egyptians towards change. They understood the universe as an equilibrium of opposites. Change, if it was of a regularly recurring type, like the succession of the seasons, was significant because it could be considered part of an unchanging scheme. But change taking the form of a singular event was considered inconsequential, a superficial and passing disturbance of the established order.

Now people who hold these views must be deeply preoccupied with the problem of death, for this supreme and inevitable change does not fit either Egyptian alternative. It is not a recurrent event and yet it is not insignificant. Human beings are too thoroughly differentiated for the elimination of any individual to appear as part of a series of recurrences. The Egyptians saw in this differentiation, this prevalence of nontypical features, a disadvantage of humanity as compared with other living beings. The animal world knew permanence; the existence of the species was in no way affected by the continual replacement of their individual members. Royalty was immune from change in a similar manner. The throne was always occupied by Horus, son of Osiris—from another viewpoint, by the son of Re. We have seen in Chapter 2 that written and pictorial documents emphasized the typical in Pharaoh, and his death caused no more than a passing agitation, without making any essential change. Pharaoh, like a large proportion of the animal world, shared permanence with the divinely ordered universe and was truly superhuman. But the death of an ordinary mortal made a change for all those who were concerned at all; it was a singular yet significant event, difficult to evaluate by Egyptian standards.

The Egyptians, like the vast majority of men, considered death an interruption, not the end, of life—a change in a man's personality, not its annihilation. Their belief in the continued existence of the dead is shown in a striking manner by the fact that in certain emergencies they addressed letters to dead relatives.[1] In one case a dead mother is asked to arbitrate between her sons, one of whom is also dead while the other is still alive. Another letter is addressed to a man whose widow and small son are beset by grasping relatives, and he is begged to "awake" his ancestors and with their help to rescue his family. We may assume that in Egypt, as elsewhere, the continued significance of the dead in the emotional and intellectual life of their survivors established the reality of their afterlife beyond a doubt; their appearance in dreams and visions confirmed it. Thus the survival of the dead belonged to the data of actual experience, and the manner of survival became a matter of great concern.

It has become a commonplace to say that the Egyptians imagined life after death as a replica of life upon earth. But this is only a partial truth and its inadequacy is generally obscured by the curious nature of our evidence. By far

[1] Alan H. Gardiner and K. Sethe, *Egyptian Letters to the Dead* (London, 1928).

the largest number of the relevant documents are concerned
with precautions which the Egyptians took to ensure existence after death; they tell us little about the nature of that
existence. Explicit statements about man's future state do
not appear before the First Intermediate period; but the
inscriptions on the coffins of that time are deeply influenced
by the Pyramid Texts composed for the kings of the Old
Kingdom, and while we shall presently explain the appearance of royal texts in private tombs, the fact remains that
we know very little about the original expectations of common men regarding an afterlife.

We do possess, however, evidence antedating by more
than a thousand years the usurped texts. This evidence consists of tombs, of which we have an unbroken series, extend-
ing from prehistoric times—probably from the fifth millennium B.C.—to the Christian era. In all these tombs the
bodies, carefully prepared and dressed, are buried with
their personal ornaments, toilet requisites, sometimes weapons or tools, and always with large numbers of pots and
dishes containing food and drink. But these supplies do not
prove that the Egyptians considered life after death a mere
continuation of life upon earth. They only show that the
Egyptians could not imagine life, in whatever form, to per-
sist while the requirements of life were superseded. The
texts confirm the fact that life after death was thought to
require sustenance in the form in which all life requires it,
as food and drink. But it is totally unwarranted to conclude
that this simple idea exhausted the Egyptian's conception
of man's future condition. It is not even correct to assume
that his supplying funerary provisions carried the materialistic implications which it inevitably suggests to us. On
the contrary, the mysterious character of life—namely, that

it is sustained by matter, although it is intangible and im-
material in itself—led the Egyptian not to a materialistic
interpretation of life, but to a spiritual view of food: the
same word, *Ka*, which denotes man's impalpable vital
force also means, in the plural, his sustenance. In the
Memphite Theology (page 23 and following, above) the
account of creation mentions immediately before the establishment of justice—therefore in a context of the highest
order—that the Ka's were created, "they that make all
sustenance and all food." The offerings at the tomb are
specifically made to a man's Ka, to his vital force. A man
who died was said "to go to his Ka," for while it was clear
that his vitality had left his body, he must needs have re-
joined the life force since he survived. All this evidence
shows, therefore, that the Egyptians held it necessary to
sustain a man's Ka, but also that this was a means to an end
—survival—not an end in itself.[2]

It is clear that we are still discussing the Egyptians' preoccupation with the possibility and conditions of survival.
And it may be admitted that many never went beyond
thoughts of this order. But definite conceptions of man's
future state did exist; and we cannot subscribe to the
prevalent view that on this subject the Egyptians held a
number of incompatible ideas in a hazy or muddleheaded
confusion. We have met similar judgments as regards the
Egyptian gods, the Egyptian myths, and so on. But we
have found on closer inspection of the evidence that the
ancients' adherence to quasi-contradictory opinions was
not due to any inability on their part to think clearly, but
to their habit of using several separate avenues of approach

[2] I have discussed the Ka at length in Chapter 5 of *Kingship and the Gods*
(Chicago, 1948).

to subjects of a problematical nature (see above, page 4 and following). They did justice to the complexity of a problem by allowing a variety of partial solutions, each of which was valid for a given approach to the central problem. The problem of life and death was considered in this manner; and we shall follow the Egyptians in discussing, one after the other, their different approaches to it. We begin with the attitude of those who were primarily concerned with the prerequisites of survival; to them survival appeared in the first place as life in the tomb.

THE DEAD IN THE TOMBS

The many-sided character of the Egyptian tomb can best be understood if we consider the trends of thought which converged on it. When the thought of a man as he was in his lifetime prevailed over all others, and the concern that he should lack nothing was uppermost in the mind, the tomb appeared as his dwelling place. Certain rock-cut tombs of the Second Dynasty are adapted to serve as his house, even to the extent of being fitted with a toilet. A spell in the "Book of the Dead" is entitled "Coming Forth by Day," in an obvious analogy with the habits of the living: the night is dangerous and eerie and man, whether alive or dead, had best stay at home. Hence a variant of the same title: "Coming Forth by Day, Receding by Night in Thy Tomb." [3] This view of a man's existence after death had more than one root. In the first place, a man's body rested in the tomb, and the Egyptians could not abstract the survival of man's immortal parts from the continued

[3] H. Kees, *Totenglauben und Jenseitsvorstellungen der alten Ägypter* (Leipzig, 1926), p. 274.

existence of his body. In this inability, as in that of imagin-
ing life independent of material sustenance, they showed
how strongly their minds were orientated towards the concrete. So, while they admitted that man suffered physical
death and nevertheless survived, they could not imagine
such a survival without a physical substratum. Man without a body seemed incomplete and ineffectual. He required
his body in perpetuity, as if it were the concrete basis of his
individuality. Hence the development of mummification
and the elaborate measures against tomb robbers who
might be attracted by ornaments and other valuables with
which the dead were equipped. Hence, also, the marvelous development of Egyptian sculpture; for a statue, properly identified with the dead man by an inscription and
magically animated by the "opening of the mouth" cere-
mony, could replace the body if it should be damaged by
decay or violence. Therefore a man was forever attached
to his tomb because his survival required preservation of
his physical form, either as mummy or as statue. This
attachment in turn strengthened the feeling, natural
enough to be universal, that at the grave one is close to
the departed; and this feeling explains also certain features
of the Egyptian tombs.

The Egyptians communicated regularly with their dead
and concretely shared their company. They visited the
tombs not only to make offerings to the Ka's, but they
gathered there on feast days for celebrations, including a
meal at which the dead were supposed to be present; this
custom has, in fact, survived in Egypt to this day. And the
tombs expressed in their architecture the fact that they
formed a link between the dead and the living. Simple
brick structures of the First Dynasty (Figure 19) show a

small walled-in space against the grave mound; in this enclosure water jars and food jars were found, the remnants
either of feasts or of regular offerings. At the same spot two
holes pierced the brickwork of the tomb, and the dead
were buried in such a way that they faced these openings.
Symbolically, at least, these served as channels of communication. The same thought found a more dignified
architectural expression in later times: a large stone slab
with a narrow groove in the middle formed the so-called
"false door" (Figure 21).[4] Behind it, underground, was
the sarcophagus chamber, where the body rested. In front
of it was the offering table upon which food and drink
were deposited. In the wall of the tomb chapel, covered
with reliefs or paintings, the false door formed the focal
point of the visitors' attention: here communication with
the dead was possible. In the Sixth Dynasty the dead man's
statue was sometimes placed in the opening of the false
door (Figure 22). But the narrow groove of the original
conception suggests more effectively the nature of contact
with the unseen which took place here; and this older
form remained in use even after the Sixth Dynasty.

In the superstructure of the tomb, passages and rooms
were covered with reliefs and paintings depicting fishing,
hunting, harvesting, and the manufacture of untold objects
of daily use. Life's necessities were thus at all times available to the dead man even if the actual offerings at the
tomb might be forgotten. But the tombs of those who
could afford it were endowed with lands, serfs, whole
villages sometimes, which were supposed to supply their
produce to the dead man in perpetuity. A mortuary priest

---

[4] Similar usages are widespread in the ancient world. See F. J. Tritsch,
"False Doors on Tombs," in *Journal of Hellenic Studies*, 63 (1943),
113–15.

recited the daily service, and certain nobles made contracts which were engraved in the tomb and which described the lands and serfs which they made over to priests, who in return obliged themselves and their descendants to perform the services of the dead and to supply offerings in specified amounts on feast days as well. Poorer people were, of course, dependent on their families. In the upheaval of the First Intermediate period (pages 84–87 above), when the transitory character of all earthly institutions had become painfully evident, the habit of relying on descendants and priests weakened and magical safeguards began to increase. Instead of (or in addition to) reliefs and paintings in accessible rooms of the tomb, wooden figures of men and women laboring at their tasks were hidden underground. Even the occasional passer-by was called upon to supply the dead man's need if he should be neglected by those bound to care for him. We read, for instance, the following prayer:

O ye who live and exist, who love life and hate death, whosoever shall pass by this tomb; as ye love life and hate death, so ye shall offer to me that which is in your hands. If nought is in your hands, ye shall speak thus with your mouth: a thousand of bread and beer, of oxen and geese, of alabaster vessels and linen, a thousand of all pure things to the revered Enyotef, son of Enyotef, son of Khuu.[5]

Summarizing, we may say that the tomb created the necessary conditions for life in the hereafter. It was a necessity to be buried properly in a well-equipped tomb, and this requirement was, for instance, emphasized when

[5] Gardiner, *The Attitude of the Ancient Egyptians to Death and the Dead* (Cambridge, 1935), p. 36. See on these "appels aux vivants" the book by Jean Sainte Fare Garnot, *L'Appel aux vivants dans les textes funéraires égyptiens,* "Recherches d'archéologie, de philologie et d'histoire," IX (Cairo, Institut Français, 1938).

King Senusert I recalled Sinuhe from his self-imposed exile:

> Come back to Egypt, that thou mayest see the Residence wherein thou didst grow up, that thou mayest kiss the earth at the Two Great Portals (the palace), and mingle with the Chamberlains.
> Even today thou hast begun to be old, thou hast lost thy manhood, and hast bethought thee of the day of burial . . .

A proper Egyptian burial is then described in alluring detail and the letter ends:

> Thus shalt thou not die abroad nor shall the Asiatics bury thee. Thou shalt not be placed in a sheep-skin. . . . Wherefore, bethink thee of thy corpse and return.[6]

The tomb was the instrument by which was overcome the disintegration of a man's personality as a result of the crisis of death. The tomb is a place of transfiguration, *sakh*, a word applied to the funerary rites, which means making the dead man an *Akh*, a transfigured spirit. The tomb contained his unchanging physical form, as a mummy and in the form of statues; it contained, in reality or in effigy, the provisions made for his *Ka*, his vital force. It offered him a basis for his existence after death; but this existence went far beyond the confines of his tomb. The conception that the dead live in their tombs was only valid in a context of preoccupation with the requirements of survival.

THE APPEARING DEAD

The dead man conceived as living an animated existence after death was called *Ba*. We translate that word, uncomfortably, with "soul," but the Ba was not a part of a living

---

[6] After Adolf Erman, *The Literature of the Ancient Egyptians*, tr. A. M. Blackman (London, 1927), pp. 23–24.

person but the whole of a person as he appears after death. The word Ba means "animation, manifestation." The Phoenix is the Ba—the manifestation—of Re. A potent amulet may be called the Ba of Shu. The Egyptians, like the Greeks, the Babylonians, and many other peoples, saw manifestations of the dead in birdlike apparitions, with thin piping voices, fluttering through the air near their former haunts. In the tomb designs the dead are depicted as birds with human heads—possibly a graphic device to distinguish them from real birds. They are sometimes supplied with arms, namely, when these are needed by the artist to clarify an action—for instance, the scooping of water from a pond near the tomb. In the great cosmological ceiling design in the cenotaph of Seti I at Abydos (Figure 10, on the right) a small oval is drawn outside the course of the sun along the sky. The oval contains three different birds and the text describes them as follows:

These birds have faces like men, but their nature is that of birds. One of them speaks to the other with words of weeping. Now after they come to eat vegetables and green stuff in Egypt, they flutter under the rays of heaven and then their shapes become bird-like.[7]

In the design the birds do not have "faces like men"; it seems the scribe was under the influence of the hieroglyphic script when he wrote this sentence. The "words of weeping" may in a similar way have slipped in as a characterization of the dead; for, notwithstanding the hope of a blessed hereafter, death was viewed as a calamity (page 108 below), and there is a common adjuration, "As you love life and hate death!" The text referring to the birds

[7] H. Frankfort, *The Cenotaph of Seti I at Abydos* (London, 1933), p. 73.

in Figure 10 is also preserved in a papyrus which has the variant phrase: "With words of men, in the language of men." [8] In any case, the dead could come to the earth and flutter under the rays of the sun in bird shape. But they did not lose contact with the tomb where the body was preserved. In this respect too they resembled the apparitions of the dead of folklore the world over. Man's complete personality after death consisted of Ba and body; the Ba-bird is often shown hovering over the body (Figure 20), or flying down the tomb shaft to rejoin it (Figure 17). In a New Kingdom papyrus occurs the phrase: "May his Ba not separate itself from his corpse forever," [9] and in the "Dialogue of a Man Weary of Life" the speaker, on the point of committing suicide, attempts to persuade his Ba to stay with him in death. Yet it was precisely as Ba that man escaped confinement in the tomb. This is shown by the text from the cenotaph of Seti I, by the designs, and also by certain spells intended to enable a man to assume any form he likes. The theme is often elaborated, and since the Ba was conceived as a bird, bird shapes are those most often named, as in the example I quote below in Dr. Gardiner's translation. Notice that the first sentence, after indicating the purpose of the spell, harks back to the interment and continues from there:

Thou shalt come in and go out, thy heart rejoicing, in the favour of the Lord of the Gods, a good burial [being thine] after a venerable old age, when age has come, thou assuming thy place in the coffin, and joining earth on the high ground of the west.

Thou shalt change into a living Ba and surely he will have

[8] After H. O. Lange and O. Neugebauer, *Papyrus Carlsberg, No. 1* (Copenhagen, 1940), p. 40.
[9] After Kees, *Totenglauben*, p. 62.

power to obtain bread and water and air; and thou shalt take shape as a heron or swallow, as a falcon or a bittern, whichever thou pleasest.

Thou shalt cross in the ferryboat and shalt not turn back; thou shalt sail on the waters of the flood, and thy life shall start afresh. Thy Ba shall not depart from thy corpse and thy Ba shall become divine with the blessed dead. The perfect Ba's shall speak to thee, and thou shalt be an equal amongst them in receiving what is given on earth. Thou shalt have power over water, shalt inhale air, and shalt be surfeited with the desires of thy heart. Thine eyes shall be given to thee so as to see, and thine ears so as to hear, thy mouth speaking, and thy feet walking. Thy arms and thy shoulders shall move for thee, thy flesh shall be firm, thy muscles shall be easy and thou shalt exult in all thy limbs. Thou shalt examine thy body and find it whole and sound, no ill whatever adhering to thee. Thine own true heart shall be with thee, yea, thou shalt have thy former heart. Thou shalt go up to the sky, and shalt penetrate the Netherworld in all forms that thou likest.[10]

This characteristic and illuminating text shows that the thought of the Ba is closely bound to the preoccupation with the necessities of the afterlife, with the conditions which make possible survival in a satisfactory manner. The designs in which the Ba occurs corroborate that statement. The thought of survival as Ba and survival in the tomb are complementary; at any rate, they are found together and evidently occurred to a man when he envisaged his own impending death and wished to prepare for it; it similarly occurred to the surviving kinsmen responsible for the well-being of their relative after his death. The thought of the Ba, like the thought of the tomb, lies under the spell of preoccupation with the conditions of the afterlife.

[10] Gardiner, *The Attitude of the Ancient Egyptians to Death and the Dead*, pp. 29–30.

THE TRANSFIGURED DEAD

But it is also possible to think about the dead with detachment and without immediate concern. In that case the Egyptians, while admitting that the dead were dependent on their tombs and were manifest as Ba's, supplemented these beliefs with a conception of wider scope. The dead were *Akhu,* "transfigured spirits." As such they were never depicted for they existed in a sphere well beyond the ken of man. The dead became Akhu through the funerary ritual, and with reference to their tombs they were called "well-equipped transfigured spirits." But while they were manifest upon earth as Ba's, they were, as Akhu, totally withdrawn from contact with humanity. They were seen at night as stars in the sky, especially in its northern part. For the circumpolar stars which never set were demonstrably immortal. This notion is old. The word *Akh* occurs in inscriptions of the First Dynasty, and the shafts of the tombs of the Old Kingdom are on the north side to enable the dead to join their companions, "the venerable ones," clustered around the heavenly pole. In the "Book of the Dead" of a later age, the connection between the dead and the stars is still known,[11] and the Pyramid Texts command categorically:

Spirit (Akh) to the sky, corpse into the earth! [12]

It is, then, a mistake to consider the notions of Ba and Akh incompatible; the dead could be manifest upon earth as Ba's, but they were Akhu in their own peculiar and exalted form of existence.

[11] L. J. Cazemier, *Oud-Egyptiese Voorstellingen Aangaande de Ziel* (Wageningen, 1930), p. 114.
[12] Pyr. 474a.

The conception of the dead as Akhu is the vaguest and most detached of all, but also that which imparts to them the greatest luster. For it incorporates them in the perennial cosmic order, it views them as partaking of eternity in the revolution of the stars round the pole of heaven. The concept of the Akhu, therefore, foreshadows an answer to the question with which this chapter started. We asked how the Egyptians, holding that only recurring change is significant change, could account for a man's death, which is an event both singular and significant. The conceptions of survival in the tomb and of manifestation as Ba do not answer that question, but the conception of the Akh indicates that the change caused by death translated man from the sphere of the insignificant to that of the significant, from an ephemeral and singular form of existence to one which was lasting and changeless. The conceptions of an afterlife in the tomb and as Ba are weighed down by care and anxiety; the fear of death, which cannot be allayed, finds expression in endless precautions. Even as a "transfigured spirit" one had to be well equipped; but if that condition was fulfilled, death meant transition from the inconsequential existence of the single human being to participation in the perennial life of the universe.

I should not be justified in presenting this synopsis of the Egyptians' most profound conception of death if it were based exclusively on our information concerning the Akhu. But the same thought has found expression in a great variety of ways. In fact, it comes to the fore whenever the funerary texts allow anything beyond the bare preoccupation with the needs of the dead to find expression. I have discussed the Akhu and the identification of the dead with the stars first of all for three reasons: it expresses the Egyptian view in a simple manner; it represents an ancient and general belief; and it lacks the curious twist which related doctrines receive as a result of the fact that they were originally applicable to Pharaoh alone.

It is, of course, highly significant that a royal doctrine could be applied to ordinary men. This was possible because a similar conception of life after death determined the traits of Pharaoh's hereafter and that of commoners. The texts obscure rather than emphasize the common elements. Since Pharaoh was the source of society's well-being, his death and future life possessed a significance far beyond that of others. It was the subject of a great deal of speculation and gave rise to many beliefs and usages which we have studied in detail elsewhere. But in order to recognize in them a trend of thought similar to that which produced the concept of the Akh, in order to understand that royal usages could be adopted by ordinary people, we must rapidly survey here the main features of Pharaoh's life after death.

THE QUASI-ROYAL DEAD

The death of a king was, in a manner characteristic of the Egyptians, glossed over in so far as it meant a change. The succession from one king to another was viewed as an unchanging mythological situation: Horus succeeded Osiris.[13] Since most kings were succeeded by their sons, actuality tallied with theology in this respect. It also agreed in the fact that the father, Osiris, disappeared definitively from the earthly scene. In the myth Osiris, murdered by Seth, was revived, but only as a power in the beyond; Horus as-

[13] The complex figure of Osiris has been discussed at length in Chapter 15 of my *Kingship and the Gods*.

sumed the throne. In actuality this was also seen to be true. The new king assumed rule as Horus; his father had coalesced at death with Osiris, the forebear and prototype of all dead kings. The king, who in life had mediated between his people and the powers in nature, merged with these powers at his death; his vitality broke forth from the earth in which he rested. As Osiris he was alive in the growing grain, in the rising waters of the Nile, in the rising moon. The Memphite Theology, discussing the burial of Osiris, bluntly states that he "became earth." Thus Pharaoh survived in the recurring manifestations of chthonic forces; and when, therefore, the Egyptians held that the common dead circled the pole as stars, their conception of man's future state did not differ in essentials from that which obtained in the case of Pharaoh.

If a common basis made it possible for beliefs regarding the royal hereafter to be applied to ordinary folk, it remains yet to explain why such a transference should actually have taken place. The explanation lies, once more, in the profound upheaval which shook the Egyptian state after the Pyramid Age. Throughout the Old Kingdom, when royal authority was absolute, it was reasonable to believe that the divine king would lead his followers into an orderly beyond. But when royalty was swept away in the First Intermediate period, there could be no reliance on individual kings, either in this life or in the hereafter. The ancient figure of Osiris, however, remained unaffected by the turmoil in the state. Established forever in the beyond, he became the king of the dead; he was addressed as follows:

> They are all thine, all those who come to thee,
> Great and small, they belong to thee;

> Those who live upon earth, they all reach thee,
> Thou art their master, there is none outside thee.[14]

The changed outlook, which made men turn from their living monarch to Osiris, the epitome of past rulers, for guidance and support beyond the grave, possessed unprecedented potentialities. For the kingly character did not separate Osiris as completely from ordinary men as it did the living Pharaoh. We remember that Rekhmire, the vizier, described his royal master as follows:

A god by whose dealings one lives, the father and mother of all men, alone by himself without an equal.

But Osiris was a passive and a suffering figure. Murdered by Seth, bewailed by Isis, he was dependent on the support of his son Horus.[15] In this dependence on his son in the all-important matter of the tomb and its equipment, Osiris resembled every Egyptian; every man could imagine his fate after death through the good services of his son to be, like that of Osiris, a blessed one. But for the mythopoeic mind analogy becomes identity; men and women began to identify themselves with Osiris in death: the man Neferhotep became Osiris-Neferhotep; the woman Mutnofert in her funerary inscriptions became Osiris-Mutnofert. The consequences of this identification were far-reaching; it made appropriate for everybody the use of texts, rites, and emblems used hitherto only in the royal funerals. The immense prestige of the royal prerogatives, their undoubted potency, led to a wholesale usurpation

---

[14] After Kees, "Aegypten," in Alfred Bertholet, ed., *Religionsgeschichtliches Lesebuch* (Tübingen, 1928), X, 17–18.

[15] This was so in the myth; it was also true on those memorable occasions when the myth became actuality, when a Pharaoh had died and had become Osiris and his funeral, with all its elaborate pomp, was the responsibility of his son, the new king, Horus. See my *Kingship and the Gods*.

by common men. Already in the First Intermediate period royal crowns and scepters began to appear among the objects depicted in the coffins of commoners as indispensable equipment for their existence after death. Soon afterwards we find that priests and acquaintances officiating at the burials of the middle class paraded the titles and costumes of the highest functionaries at the courts of the pyramid builders: hereditary prince, treasurer of the god (= king), royal kinsman, and so on. Another consequence was a greatly increased prestige of the cemeteries at Abydos, where Osiris was supposed to be buried. It was impractical for most people to endow a tomb and a funerary priest away from their native city where their descendants could take care of the regular offerings. But it was possible to erect a small cenotaph or funerary stela at Abydos, by means of which one could be imagined to be buried there to join the god, as it were, at the very beginning of one's journey into the beyond.

THE DEAD IN THE COSMIC CIRCUIT

The complexities and the manifold formalities deriving from the identification of all the dead with Osiris have obscured its most important feature: it was, once again, a means to an end, the surest way to a blessed existence beyond the grave. And once more preoccupations and anxieties prevail in the relevant texts, causing innumerable complications. For instance, it is quite usual to find a prayer to Osiris in the inscriptions of a man who calls himself Osiris-such-and-such. But the meaning of the identification is nevertheless clear: Osiris lived in the annual sprouting of the grain, in the floodwaters of the Nile, in the moon, in Orion; the dead, by becoming Osiris, acquired immor-

tality within the perennial movements of nature; and this
ideal was of immemorial antiquity in Egypt since it was
expressed from the earliest times in the wish to become
Akhu, transfigured spirits, circling as "imperishable stars
round the pole." The same ideal found yet another expression when the dead desired to join the sun in its daily
journey. This desire is strongly represented in the Pyramid
Texts of the kings of the Old Kingdom, but in the Coffin
Texts of the First Intermediate period commoners also
wish

to enter and leave by the Eastern Gate of Heaven in the retinue
of Re.

Whether the dead man's aim is the solar circuit, or that of
the circumpolar stars, or the life of Osiris, the essential
wish is the same: to be absorbed in the great rhythm of the
universe. Even in the Pyramid Texts the king joins the sun
on his downward journey in the West, where he enters
the nether world and where Osiris is. The following stanza
of a text too full of theological allusions to be quoted here
at length renders with its rhythm and repetitions the
regular, recurring, grandiose movement in which the dead
king takes part:

Thou risest and settest, thou goest down with Re, sinking in the
    dusk with Nedy;
Thou risest and settest, thou risest up with Re, and ascendest
    with the great reed float;
Thou risest and settest, thou goest down with Nephthys, sinking
    in the dusk with the evening bark of the sun;
Thou risest and settest; thou risest up with Isis, ascending with
    the morning bark of the sun.[16]

The stanza loses some of its effect when its soothing repe-

[16] *Kingship and the Gods,* p. 121; Pyr. 207–12.

titious movement is not offset by the verses which precede it in the original. Notice that, even in this old text, Isis and Nephthys, who belong to the cycle of Osiris, take part in the sun's journey, as they do in the paintings of the New Kingdom. The antagonism which is claimed to have existed between a so-called "religion of Osiris" and a "sun-religion" is a modern construction without solid foundation in the ancient texts. Underneath the endless details of diverging local usages, traditions, and beliefs, there is essential unity in the conviction that man can find immortality and peace by becoming part of one of the perennial cyclic rhythms of nature. Hence the use of the phrase "repeating life," *uhm ankh,* which is so often found. The essential unity of the different images in which life after death was comprehended is well expressed in the following blessing addressed by a god to a king:

I grant thee, that thou mayest rise like the sun, rejuvenate thyself like the moon, repeat life like the flood of the Nile.[17]

We meet, then, once again a paradox: The Egyptians, who conceived the world as static, conceived their future condition as perennial movement. But it was the recurring movement that was part of the established and unchanging order of the world.

It is possible to read through countless funerary texts without recognizing the idea which we have here formulated. Most of the texts do not rise above the level of anxious concern with the fulfillment of the requirements of survival. Others express the fear of death in peculiar images; for instance, the thought that the sun passes every night through the netherworld does not lead to the con-

17 After A. de Buck, *De godsdienstige Beteekenis van de Slaap,* "Ex Oriente Lux," Mededeelingen en Verhandelingen No. 4 (Leiden, 1939).

clusion that night there must be the equivalent of day
upon earth. The thought of darkness prevails; the sun is
thought to give but short joy to the inhabitants, and when
the iron doors close with a crash behind Re it is said that
there is general weeping among the dead. Sometimes fear
destroys faith altogether, especially in texts put in the
mouth of mourners whose grief overpowers reflection. So
we read in a song in which a widow bewails the loss of
her husband:

How sad is the descent in the Land of Silence. The wakeful
sleeps, he who did not slumber at night lies still forever. The
scorners say: The dwelling-place of the inhabitants of the West
is deep and dark. It has no door, no window, no light to illumi-
nate it, no north wind to refresh the heart. The sun does not rise
there, but they lie every day in darkness. . . . The guardian has
been taken away to the Land of Infinity.

Those who are in the West are cut off, and their existence is
misery; one is loath to go to join them. One cannot recount one's
experiences but one rests in one place of eternity in darkness.[18]

But even if we ignore here such bypaths, even if we disregard all texts which only express anxiety or describe precautions, we shall never find the plain statement that man
will find blessedness as an immortal participant in the
rhythm of natural life. For such a formula possesses a degree of abstraction which is totally unknown to Egyptian
thought. Nevertheless, it expresses well enough the common denominator of the various imaginative conceptions
which alone possessed significance for the Egyptians: joining the sun in his boat, joining the circumpolar stars, re-
juvenation with the moon or with Osiris. If we take these
images literally they are as inadequate as that of the blessed

[18] After Kees, in *Zeitschrift für aegyptische Sprache,* 62 (1927), 73–79.

m Paradise playing lutes before the throne of God. We must, in either case, grasp the mood, and translate in abstract terms the expectation which the images embody. In doing so, we destroy the directness and the emotional complexity which form the force and beauty—in fact, the *raison d'être*—of those images. To repeat an example given in the first chapter: Where the sunset is inseparable from the thought of death, the dawn is a surety of resurrection. The relevancy of the natural phenomena to human problems is a matter of direct experience, not of intellectual argument. It is an intuitive insight, not a theory. It induces faith, not knowledge. And this gives us yet another reason why the texts seem to ignore the conception we formulated. The texts have, to a large extent, a practical purpose; they are intended to supply the dead with knowledge which he may require on his journey; they do not express his expectations.

Nevertheless, it is remarkable that the aim of the journey, the abode of the dead, is hardly described at all; the few phrases speaking of a hereafter containing fields of barley with ears five cubits high can be recognized as secondary, as we shall see. The alternative descriptions of a dark and horrible netherworld are figments of fear, not of expectation. We do not find in Egyptian texts a description of Elysian fields or even of a Plain of Asphodels, neither a Valhalla nor an Island of the Blessed. This absence of definition of the hereafter is in keeping with the conception we have found to underlie the various images of life after death: there was no land of the dead to be described. The dead lived in the great cosmic circuit of sun and stars. They lived in the sky but also below the horizon, in the netherworld; they descended in the West and rose in the East. They maintained at the same time some connection with their tomb, and through it, with life upon earth. But their lasting happiness lay beyond the earth and the tomb.

When it was necessary to refer to the region where the dead dwell, and when the words "Heaven" or "Netherworld" were avoided, the term used is "Reed Field" or "Field of Rushes." An alternative name (even by the Fifth Dynasty in a private tomb) is "Field of Offerings." This name seems odd for a place of lasting life, but it merely indicates that one must be "well equipped" to survive at all. It also shows, once again, that the ideas we discussed in connection with the tomb were not considered incompatible with the conception that immortality was found in the "harmony of the spheres." The more usual name, "Field of Rushes," has a curiously ancient and primitive ring. It ignores the agricultural life which was characteristic of Egypt in historical times—let alone the city life which was so important in the New Kingdom. It refers to the primeval scenery of the Nile Valley which was independent of the labor of man and which played a predominant part in the religious imagination of the Egyptians (page 154 below). It is appropriate to recall here that the great mother-goddess Hathor, who is known even on a predynastic slate palette, was not merely imagined in the form of a cow, but in the primitive form of a wild cow, living in the papyrus marshes and appearing to the faithful when she parted the stalks with her head (Figure 25). It is, then, perfectly clear that the conception of a "Field of Rushes" as the land of the dead belongs to the oldest stratum in Egyptian religion. In contrast therewith the artificial nature of the following picture is evi-

dent: on a coffin from Assiut we find a description of the
Field of Rushes, in one of the common texts by means
of which the dead man may gain favored treatment from
the powers of the Hereafter by knowledge of their secrets:

I know the Field of Rushes; its enclosure wall is made of metal;
the height of its Lower Egyptain corn is four cubits, one cubit
the ear and three cubits the stem. . . . The East dwellers
harvest there, each nine cubits tall. . . .[19]

The total discrepancy between this Gargantuan harvest
and the name of the place, "Field of Rushes," shows it up
for one of those pieces of verbiage with which the funerary texts pad out ideas incapable of meaningful elaboration. This text survives in the "Book of the Dead" and
it even inspired tomb paintings in the Nineteenth and
Twentieth dynasties. It is more instructive to return to
the original idea, the Field of Rushes. It is a place one
passes through, and it really stands for the dynamic Hereafter which we have described. This is stated in the Pyramid Texts, for instance:

Heaven was pregnant of thee, together with Orion;
The morning bore thee together with Orion.
[Since he] lives who lives by order of the gods,
Thou shalt live.
Thou risest with Orion in the eastern part of Heaven;
Thou settest with Orion in the western part of Heaven.
The third of you (that is, your companion) is the Dog Star, of
    the pure places,
It is she who will guide you on the beautiful roads
Which are in Heaven, in the Field of Rushes.[20]

This text (and it does not stand alone) [21] leaves no doubt
as to the context and meaning of the Field of Rushes. In

[19] After Kees, "Aegypten," in *Religionsgeschichtliches Lesebuch*, p. 52
(Book of the Dead, Ch. 109).
[20] Pyr. 821–22.   [21] For example, Pyr. 2062.

the Coffin Texts a vulgarized rendering of the same conception occurs:

> I pass through Heaven, I walk upon Nut;
> My mansion is in the Field of Rushes,
> My riches are in the Field of Offerings.[22]

One may hazard a guess as to the association of ideas which made the "Field of Rushes" appear to be an appropriate name for the dynamic Hereafter of the Egyptians. The main impulse which leads man to depict to himself his future state is fear. The conviction that man survives death does not diminish the fear of death; both were primary data of experience to the Egyptian but when he came to depict survival, in words or images, fear generally prevailed. The same is true almost everywhere, and the fear of death habitually finds expression in imagined obstacles on the road towards blessedness. For instance, there is an almost world-wide belief that the dead have to cross water. In Egypt this is one of the commonest themes. The names of the obstacles are illuminating: the Winding Lake, the Lake of the Thousand Water Birds, and the Lake of the Jackal—but also the Lake of Rushes and the Lake of Dawn. The Field of Rushes is an obvious part of this scenery (Figure 24); one either crosses it on the way to the water or one lands in the "field" after crossing. Hence the Field of Rushes appears as the place one passes through on the "right way," the way of the cosmic circuit, in the following Pyramid Text:

Pepi has come that he may purify himself in the Field of Rushes;
He descends to the Field of Kenset;[23]

[22] After Kees, *Totenglauben*, p. 289.
[23] This name of the field refers to the "source" of the Nile in the whirlpools of the First Cataract where the water just emerging from Nun, the primeval ocean still existing below the earth, was the purest.

The followers of Horus purify Pepi,
They bathe him, they dry him,
They recite for him the Spell of the Right Way;
They recite for him the Spell of Ascent.
Pepi ascends to Heaven.
He embarks in the boat of Re.
Pepi commands for him (Re) the gods who row him.
All the gods are jubilant at the approach of Pepi
As they are jubilant at the approach of Re,
When he emerges at the eastern side of Heaven,
In peace, in peace.

The Field of Rushes is the natural imaginative complement to the watery obstacle which the dead man has
to cross. In this quotation it is a place of purification from
which he ascends to Heaven. In the preceding quotation,
also from the Pyramid Texts (page 111), the Field of
Rushes was identical with Heaven, the place of the "beautiful roads" upon which the dead king would go with
Orion, guided by the Dog Star. The Field of Rushes does
not, then, possess any particular location; it may be invoked as the place where the dead are in connection with
any part of the solar and astral circuit which happens to
be discussed. It would seem, perhaps, that so concrete a
term as the "Field of Rushes" cannot possibly designate
the circuit. But our last quotation illustrates very clearly
the associative origin of such images; as soon as the dead
king's ascent to Heaven is mentioned, the thought of the
sun-boat which daily crosses the sky arises; and the image
of the boat, in its turn, calls up that of its crew of rowers;
next, King Pepi is given his place within the detailed picture as foreman of the crew. We seem far removed from
the basic thought that immortality is found when man
merges in the life of nature. But the text has merely in-

sisted on its theme, and since the Egyptian mind always tends towards the concrete, its insistence leads to the elaboration of a concrete image which strikes us as distracting. But the hymn returns to the main theme in the concluding lines, when it says that the gods jubilate at Pepi's appearance as they jubilate when Re appears at the eastern horizon. Since comparisons possess for the mythopoeic mind the force of identifications, the concluding lines amount to a different form of the statement that Pepi has joined the sun's circuit, which was also implied by the image of the sun-boat and crew. The Field of Rushes is, in a similar way, a product of association, which starts with the Lake of Rushes as the oldest known expanse of water in Egypt.

If the thought prevails that the dead man joins the sun, the watery obstacle becomes the Lake of Dawn from which the sun rises. But the water from which the sun rises up is also Nun, the primeval ocean, from which he rose on the day of creation and which since then has surrounded and supported the earth created in its midst. This was a logical thought, since the primeval ocean possessed an immense potential of life, and the water upon which the life of Egypt depended was tapped, as subsoil water, in wells; or it rose from below the earth in the eddies and whirlpools of the First Cataract, where the Nile and the inundation were thought to originate. The water to be crossed can therefore be conceived as the primeval ocean, and the aim is the Isle of Flame where the sun rose at the creation of the world. Hence the following odd text, on a papyrus of the First Intermediate period:

These transfiguration-spells which are to be performed for the well-equipped and justified X (name of the deceased), who is in his tomb, are intended to enable him to establish his household on the Isle of Flames.[24]

If one has to cross the primeval waters in death, and these are below the earth, too, there is no inconsistency if one is supposed to descend into one's tomb in order to cross these waters in the netherworld. The sun too descends at dusk and passes the netherworld before ascending at dawn. The whole cosmic circuit, over the earth and under the earth, is, if you like, "the land of the dead." Descending into the grave one joins the sun in his nightly course; the tomb is an essential part of the circuit. During the funerary procession the crossing of the Nile is performed,[25] an act of sympathetic magic intended to support the dead man's effort. A text explaining a boat journey depicted in an Old Kingdom tomb mentions a Delta city as the starting point and the Field of Rushes as the aim of the journey: "Coming from Buto and sailing to the Field of Offerings." [26] Man's journey to the tomb merges without a break into the path on which sun and stars move perennially, the "beautiful roads upon which walk the venerated dead." The quasi-rational suggestion that these roads, also called "the roads of the West," are merely the roads from a man's house to his tomb, is absurd. We have seen that they are, among other things, roads in Heaven (page 111). The references to these roads come mostly from Old Kingdom tombs, but even in the Eighteenth Dynasty we find texts like the following as the legend to a picture showing the funerary procession:

Making a goodly burial for . . . Amenemhet . . . causing the god (that is, the dead man) to ascend unto his horizon, conduct-

24 After Kees, *Totenglauben*, p. 335.
25 Wilson, in *Journal of Near Eastern Studies*, III (1944), 201–18.
26 After Hermann Junker, *Giza*, II (Vienna and Leipzig, 1934), 67.

ing him to the shaft of the Necropolis in peace, in peace, beside the great god. Proceeding in peace to the sky, to the horizon, to the [Field of Reeds], to the Underworld, to the Hall, or to the place wherever(?) he is.[27]

Here, then, the circuit is still mentioned, with its main elements as they were known already in the Old Kingdom. And the text explicitly states that the road to the tomb leads to the great circuit embracing sky, horizon, the Field of Rushes, and the netherworld. The consistency and also the lasting significance of this conception of life after death cannot be doubted. But we must be prepared to find it overgrown, and often enough obliterated, by thoughts which the never-allayed fear of death called forth. For this fear oppresses man without respite, and he finds an outlet in the creation of images which may be horrible but which have, at least, the advantage of being definite. Moreover, they do not depict a lasting state of wretchedness but dangers and obstacles which may be overcome. However, since the fear of death remains, the obstacles show a tendency to multiply themselves. If there is water to cross, there must be a ferryman. If one imagines a closed Hereafter there must be a gate with a porter. But the ferryman or the porter may be a bully, or may insist on payment, or on a password, and so on. One arms oneself as best one can with magical spells; one pretends to be an important person, for whom the gods are waiting; or one pretends that one is a god oneself. So one says to the porter or the ferryman or the Cerberus in whatever shape he appears:

Thou uncircumcised one, leave the road free for me. I am the Great Male looking for the Great Female. I have come to look

[27] After Alan H. Gardiner and Nina de Garis Davies, *The Tomb of Amenemhet* (London, 1915), p. 49.

for that lock of Re-Atum which was taken away on that day of
rebellion.

Or another one:

X has come to you pure as Khnumis (a decan star), free of bad
defects. X has come to you that you should open for him, Porter;
that you should unlock for him, Great Bolt! Let this Osiris-X see
Re in his form, so that he may hear what X has to say to him;
and bring Thoth on the job and Seshat on the job, so that they
can give him that document and that knowledge and that transfiguration of the Island of Flames. X has power over them, so
that he can see those who are there among the honored
ones.[28]

There is no end to spells of this type; fear and precaution
combine in a chain reaction in which each newly formed
security disintegrates by the apprehension of a new danger.
The Coffin Texts and the "Book of the Dead," the "Book
of Gates" and, in fact, the whole funerary literature of
Egypt, is a literature of the fear of death. One of the
imagined dangers is a judgment in the hereafter.

We must distinguish the ancient texts in which evildoers
are warned that they will be called to judgment before the
Great God (page 95) from the judgment of the late
funerary papyri. The old inscriptions are in keeping with
the general conviction that the gods insist upon Maat—
order, justice, truth—and that those who move against it
are doomed. The same feeling finds expression in the letters addressed to the dead, to which we have referred
(page 89). Whether the Great God of the Old Kingdom
inscriptions represents the king, Re, or Osiris, is imma-
terial. All of these vindicated Maat. But just because the
Egyptians believed justice and truth to be part of the cos-

[28] After Kees, *Totenglauben*, p. 276.

mic order, there could be no question of a judgment of all the dead in the sense which biblical religion gives to that conception. For the Egyptian the righteous man was in harmony with the divine order, and there the matter ended. This view, which does away with a formal judgment altogether, has great dignity. So, for instance, in the "Instructions for King Merikare":

Put not thy faith in length of years, for the gods regard a lifetime as but an hour. A man remains over after reaching the haven of death. His deeds are laid beside him for all treasure. Eternal is the existence yonder. A fool is he who has made light of it. But he who has reached it without wrongdoing, shall continue yonder like a god, stepping forward boldly like the Lords of Eternity.[29]

The forty-two judges of the late funerary papyri belong to an entirely different order of thought. They are simply another obstacle to be passed. Like those other dangers and obstructions which we have discussed, they were created by fear, assisted, in this case, by an uneasy conscience. The forty-two judges are overcome in exactly the same way as the monsters with knives, the bullying porters and ferrymen, and so forth, namely, by magic. People take care that they are buried with a papyrus containing the "Declaration of Innocence." In this they state emphatically that they have done nothing wrong whatsoever. They furthermore take with them a spell—often written on a large scarab—to prevent their own hearts from rising up and bearing witness against them.

All matters concerned with the formal judgment of the dead are on a similarly low level, and cannot be con-

---

[29] After Gardiner, in *Journal of Egyptian Archaeology*, I (1914), 27, ll. 55–57.

sidered on a par with the serious preoccupations with righteousness which we discussed in the preceding chapter. I merely mention the judgment here because many scholars, in their anxiety to make the ancient Egyptian appear like one of us, have laid great stress on this "judgment of the dead" as evidence of his advanced ethical standards. As we have seen, the Egyptians were firmly convinced that one should live according to common human decency, and that those acts which we too call evil lead to disaster. But his fear of the forty-two judges of the netherworld is in line with his fear that he might forget his name or that he might have to walk upside down, or to eat dirt, or, for that matter, be forced to work. I mention this last fear because in all public and private collections of Egyptian antiquities you will find Ushebtis, little mummy-shaped figurines, generally holding a hoe, which were compelled by the spell written upon them to answer a possible call for labor on behalf of the dead man who had bought them:

O thou, Ushebti, if Osiris-X is assigned to do any work that is done in the other world . . . to cultivate the fields, to irrigate the banks, to transport sand of the East and of the West,—"Lo, here I am! " shalt thou say.[30]

The anxiety of the Egyptian in the face of death gives a rather striking foil to the serenity of his positive beliefs in a future life. The conflict between these two moods is expressed in a dialogue between Atum, the creator, and Osiris. I can only quote the beginning because the text is, as usual, full of theological allusions which would require long comments to be understandable. Osiris clearly rep-

[30] T. George Allen, *Handbook of the Egyptian Collections in the Art Institute of Chicago* (Chicago, 1920), p. 62.

resents the ordinary man, contemplating with fear the prospects of his future life; Atum explains the cosmic order of his own creation in which death has its appointed place:

Osiris said: O Atum, what does this mean that I must go into the desert? It has no water, it has no air, it is very deep, very dark, boundless.

(Atum:) You will live there without care.

(Osiris:) But one cannot find there the satisfaction of love.

Atum said: I have put there transfiguration in the place of water, air and satisfaction; and carefreeness in the place of bread and beer.[31]

The identification with Osiris had, then, gone so far that he is made to voice man's fears. Atum propounds the view that immortality is transfiguration to a participation in the life of his cosmos which even dispenses with the requirements of sustenance. Our text is exceptional in this as in other respects. And it is understandable that the ordinary man, absorbed by the struggle for existence in his lifetime, did not think much beyond the measures of precaution which usage indicated as desirable in case of his death. It is this limited, worried point of view which prevails in so many texts; and it is this point of view which appears as a mechanical projection of ordinary life into the beyond. And so we read in the "Book of the Dead" [32] that the dead man "enters and leaves the Netherworld and lives in the Field of Rushes, the wide windy place. He is powerful there and transfigured, he ploughs there and harvests

[31] After Kees, "Aegypten," in *Religionsgeschichtliches Lesebuch*, p. 27; E. Naville, *Proceedings of the Society of Biblical Archaeology* (London, 1904); Book of the Dead, Ch. 175.

[32] After Erman, *Die Religion der Aegypter; ihr Werden und Vergehen in vier Jahrtausenden* (Berlin and Leipzig, 1934), p. 229.

there and drinks there and loves there and does everything he had done upon earth." And in a Coffin Text there
is a spell which grandiloquently identifies a dead man
with "the son of Atum, the comrade of Truth," but which
has the simple and attractive superscription: "[Spell] to
build a house for a man in the Land of the Dead, to cultivate the fields, and to plant fruit trees." [33]

It is no wonder that those who approach Egyptian religion from such adaptations, and take their stand on texts
written for the least thoughtful section of the population,
reach the conclusion that the Egyptian beliefs concerning
afterlife do not make sense. But they act like a man who
would gauge our present knowledge of the stars by studying horoscopes in the newspapers. The view which we
have described in this chapter stands at the opposite end
of the scale; in fact, the belief that immortality is found
in sharing the perennial movements of nature may seem
to us too vague and too unrelated to the actual problems
of human life to qualify as a basic faith. But we must remember two circumstances in this connection.

The Egyptians lived in very close contact with nature
and found (as we have seen) in the recurring events of
the farmer's year experiences pregnant with meaning beyond the sphere of usefulness. We must allow for their
deep emotional involvement in such natural phenomena
as the sun's course or the rise and fall of the Nile. In the
second place, the one-sidedness of any belief could find
a corrective in other views held simultaneously. We have
repeatedly referred to this "multiplicity of approaches"
and it is relevant now when yet another attitude of the
Egyptians towards death is to be indicated. I ignored this

[33] After Kees, *Totenglauben*, pp. 283–84.

particular attitude when I stated (page 94) that the scenes in the tombs merely served to supply the dead with their material requirements. The statement was true as far as it went but it did not exhaust the significance of Egyptian funerary art. It ignored the fact that art is expression in form, and in the Egyptian tomb paintings and reliefs an attitude towards death becomes articulate which I shall now indicate by quoting from a forthcoming work by Mrs. Frankfort, *Time and Space in the Representational Art of the Ancient Near East*. The passage occurs where scenes painted in the tombs of the New Kingdom are discussed:

The central concept which gives these scenes their unity . . . , the metaphysical problem that lay at the root of all Egyptian funerary art, was the problem of the relation between life and death. Seen in the light of this problem, the different types of scenes are merely various approaches, varying answers, but all imply the same assertion that death is a mere phase of life, that the significance of life is as timeless as death. These scenes are quite literally concerned with eternal values, namely, the immanent values of life such as power, wealth, abundance seen *sub specie aeternitatis*. . . . The essential value of political power was expressed in the relation between the high official and the divine head of state; wealth implied in the first place the subtle beauty of conviviality with music, poetry, and dance; and abundance meant throughout, not only the possession of goods and a surfeit of food, but a joyful awareness of earth's fecundity, of beasts and plants and the infinite variety of man's labor. These scenes contain an implicit but emphatic denial that death should be a tragic and violent negation of life; on the contrary, they attempt a harmonious approximation, a mutual interpenetration of life and death on a scale never equalled by any other people. It is true that death, the unknown, claimed ever present awareness and unceasing service on the part of the living; but this was not merely the price at which doubt and terror could be kept at bay, but a tribute paid to the phenomena of life which, pictured in a funerary setting, became unassailable even by death.

All attempts to make the strangeness of this very mature art less alien by "reading" it like a trivial story are attempts to rob it of its dignity and its truly religious character. And this is all the more deplorable because the paradox of the oneness of life and death is balanced on a knife's edge between childish wish-bound thought and profound resignation, between the hope that life's pleasures might last and the recognition that life is eternal only through death.

5

Change and Permanence in Literature and Art

THE number of paradoxes which we have met in these chapters gives a fair measure of the distance which separates us from the ancient Egyptians. We found that they viewed their state as but the sphere of action of their king, an absolute and quasi-omnipotent monarch; yet their documents do not enable us to recognize a single Pharaoh as a distinct personality. They lived under the direct rule of a god, yet they were without divine guidance in their daily lives. They denied the reality of death, yet they were perpetually preoccupied with it and spent a large part of their substance in preparing for its occurrence.

In the field of artistic and literary expression with which we must deal now, equally baffling situations occur. Egyptian art reproduced the innumerable details of the people's lives with obvious relish, yet it differentiated its renderings consistently from direct visual impressions. In Egyptian literature royalty plays an altogether preponderant part; even the popular tales chose it for their subject matter; yet the epic, which everywhere else celebrates royal deeds, was practically unknown in Egypt. For our present purpose we shall summarize these paradoxes in the fields of literature and art in a single one: The Egyptians invented many of the forms of expression which remained significant forever afterwards, yet they rarely realized the potentialities which their discoveries have since appeared to possess.

We have seen in the preceding chapters that similar paradoxes are dissolved by a more penetrating study of the evidence. Once they have put us on our guard, once we remember that we can take nothing for granted and that conceptions which are familiar—or even axiomatic—to us, may be irrelevant to ancient culture, it becomes clear that the paradoxes are founded on a discrepancy between our own outlook and the views and intentions of the ancients. We must ask, therefore, whether this is also true in the case of literary and artistic expression, and whether the peculiar attitude of mind of the Egyptians, which we recognized in studying their gods, their state, their way of life, and their views of immortality, can also be recognized in what they left us when we consider those documents as vehicles of artistic expression.

We shall start by considering Egyptian literature and we exclude, of course, all texts which are merely informative. For we have to deal, in Webster's words, with "writings distinguished by artistic form or emotional appeal." But we are severely handicapped by the system of writing which the Egyptians invented. They did not write vowels but only the consonantal skeletons of words. Learned research has been able to reconstruct to some extent the vocalization and accentuation of Egyptian, but for our purpose the language in its physical reality of sound and rhythm is lost. And without these musical elements a judgment of literary achievement would seem impossible. This is certainly true as regards lyric poetry. The love songs, work songs, and other short pieces which have been preserved offer little hold to literary criticism. But this is not so where the larger compositions are concerned. We can recognize some highly organized poetic forms, and although our knowledge is lamentably incomplete, we may attempt a formal criticism of the Egyptians' literary output.

But at the very outset we meet yet another difficulty: We cannot apply our literary categories. The three types of poetry which predominate in the ancient literatures with which we are familiar are absent in Egypt. We can find neither myth nor epic nor drama as an art form.

THE MYTH IN FOLK TALE AND LITERATURE

The most popular myth among the Egyptians was that of Osiris, Isis, and Horus. Yet it is not known as a connected story before Plutarch recorded it. It was not, however, a late invention; both the Pyramid Texts and the Memphite Theology, of the third millennium B.C., refer to it in many places. In hymns we find the main episodes of the myth alluded to, and it is therefore all the more remarkable that it is never told coherently in religious poetry. Straightforward narration must have been common, of course, to make the allusions understandable, even to Egyptians. But such story-telling was not the concern of literature but of folk art. We know this because the coherent myths preserved in writing bear every indication of belonging to the repertoire of the popular story-tellers. They lack the accomplishments not only of Egyptian poetry, but even of the short stories which we shall discuss presently. The myths as written down are really vulgarizations of mythical lore, as regards both form and contents. The episodes follow one another without elegance: "then . . . and then . . . and then"! The contents are adapted to the story-teller's necessity of retaining the attention of his audience in the market place. The story is therefore often interrupted by some marvelous detail. For instance, a tale mentioning the sun-god digresses as follows: "His Majesty (namely, the god Re) had become old, and his bones were of silver, his flesh of gold, his hair of true lapis lazuli." This digression has a recognizable theological starting point; gold, the untarnishing metal, is called "the flesh of the gods," but the rest seems to aim at calling forth those soft exclamations of delight by which even today the public rewards a successful story-teller in the East.

The quotation also shows that the gods are humanized as much as possible in these myths, a treatment which must of necessity exceed the bonds of accepted theology, as it was described in our first chapter. In the myths as told, the interest does not center on the gods' manifestations as natural powers but on such characteristics and actions as can be understood in human terms. The sun-god has become old and wants to withdraw from his troublesome human subjects. Or he asks a lion-goddess to destroy them but regrets it when she proves really efficient; so he orders seven thousand jars of beer to be stained red, and when poured out at dawn, "the fields were covered four hands deep through the power of the majesty of this god. In the morning the goddess came and found the place flooded. Her face looked handsome in it (the red liquid). So she drank and she liked it; she got drunk and did not recognize the people."

Among the popular narratives of myths which have been preserved the cycle of Osiris is represented by the Papyrus Chester Beatty No. 1, called "The Contendings of Horus and Seth." [1] It deals with the last phase of the myth when Horus, son of Osiris and Isis, brought up in secret by his mother, has come of age and presents his claim to his father's heritage, the kingship over Egypt, before the gods. Seth, the murderer of Osiris, opposes the claim. The sun-god, presiding over the court, favors Seth, and the other gods do not know what to do or, rather, they procrastinate because the most powerful among them is not truly impartial. They ask several gods who are not present for their opinion, but each pronouncement gives rise to new disagreement. Seth says: "Let him come outside with me, then I shall show you that my hands are stronger than his." At another time Seth refuses to appear before the court when Isis is there, so the court adjourns to an island but Isis enters in disguise. In another scene a little god jeers at the sun-god in the manner of a street urchin: "Your chapel is empty," meaning, "nobody takes notice of you anyhow." The other gods throw him out, but the sun-god retires in a huff and sulks until Hathor, by a somewhat indelicate act, restores his temper. So ruses and obscene jokes succeed one another and several ancient myths are drawn upon in the course of the narrative; it reaches its conclusion when Osiris writes a letter from the netherworld threatening to charge his dreadful messengers with driving the whole court before them to the land of the dead. The verdict is then given in favor of Horus.

Now we cannot dispose of this story as an exceptionally scurrilous tale; fragments of its contents are preserved in

[1] Alan H. Gardiner, *The Chester Beatty Papyri, No. 1* (London, 1931).

other documents which antedate the papyrus by several centuries. The story-teller's repertoire was no less traditional than that of the priestly scribe with this difference (to judge by modern analogies): that the folk-tale tradition was an oral one. But if the details were frequently elaborated beyond the teachings of orthodoxy, the main features were not tampered with. It is characteristic, for instance, that at the end of the "Contendings" Seth is not destroyed. His bonds are removed and he is allowed to be with the sun-god in the sky where he can thunder— "and people will be afraid of him," adds the papyrus. This addition is typical of the folk tale; in the official texts Seth is indeed manifest in storms, but in the tale where he appears as the villain, the noisy display of power is granted him as a sop to save his self-esteem and to make him abide by the decision of the court that Horus shall succeed Osiris. The subtle teaching that opposing forces were in equilibrium in the universe could not be conveyed in a popular story, but the tenor of the tale is in keeping with the official doctrine that Horus and Seth are "reconciled."

The folk tales stand outside literature in the sense of *belles-lettres,* but their existence made it possible for the poets to allude freely to mythological events. The interesting point lies in the manner in which the poets did it. To appreciate this I shall summarize a part of the Osiris myth as related, with greater detail than I can give here, by Plutarch. Seth had murdered Osiris and thrown his coffined body into the Nile. Isis mourned and went from place to place to recover it. She found it, partly revived Osiris, and conceived Horus, whom she brought up in the marshes until he was strong enough to press his claims.

In Pharaonic times we find the fullest reference to this

part of the myth in a New Kingdom hymn to Osiris.[2] It starts in the usual manner:

> Praise to thee, Osiris! Thou Lord of Eternity,

and then continues with a series of incantations:

> He that went to rest in Herakleopolis
>
> .   .   .
>
> He whose name endureth in the mouth of men
>
> .   .   .
>
> He that established Maat throughout the land

and after a number of strophes it addresses Isis in a similar way. But in doing so it evokes Isis' action after the death of Osiris:

> Beneficent Isis, that protected her brother, that sought for him without wearying, that traversed this land mourning, and took no rest until she found him!
>
> She that afforded him shade with her feathers, and with her wings created air. She that cried aloud for joy and brought her brother to land.
>
> She that revived the faintness of the Weary One, that took in his seed and provided an heir, that suckled the child in solitude, the place where he was being unknown; that brought him, when his arm was strong, into the Hall of Geb . . .

The hymn then continues to describe in the same manner, with apostrophes, Horus' vindication by the gods; and it ends with congratulatory praise of Osiris. It therefore covers the whole section of the myth which I have summarized on the basis of Plutarch's account, and also the episode elaborated with such broad humor in the Papyrus Chester Beatty No. 1. But the hymn avoids throughout the narrative form. There is no story, no progression of

[2] After Adolf Erman, *The Literature of the Ancient Egyptians*, tr. A. M. Blackman (London, 1927), pp. 141 ff.

events, but simply a series of invocations, which one may view as varying approaches to the unique theme, the glorification of Osiris, Isis, and Horus. Each detail of the story supplies a starting point for fresh praise: "Beneficent Isis, that protected her brother . . . She that afforded him shade . . . She that revived his faintness . . ." There is not even a proper order of the episodes. In the first strophe Isis finds Osiris, yet in the second strophe she is once more presented at this turning point in her quest, for she is said to have "cried aloud and brought him to land." Every feature of the treatment shows that the poet found no inspiration at all in the actual course of events; the story as such meant nothing to him. He was, on the other hand, moved to poetry when he considered the unchanging relation between worshiper and god; he expressed himself in the static form of the hymn of praise; in other words, he expressed an unchanging, always significant, attitude.

The best proof that this anti-epical attitude towards mythological subjects was typical of Egyptian literature is the absence of a coherent account of creation. This is truly astonishing, for creation was, as we have seen, the only nonrecurrent event which the Egyptians acknowledged as significant (pages 20 and following; 50 and following). It had, in fact, made the difference between the nothingness of chaos and the fullness of existence in a divinely ordered cosmos. But the Egyptians were so little prepared to dwell on any change, that they did not even describe in orderly and continuous fashion the supreme change which took place at what they called "the first time." We are obliged to reconstruct the creation story from allusions which are frequent and from certain learned commentaries, of which we quoted one before (page 52). And yet the contemporaries of the Egyptians left us not only the story of Genesis, but also the Babylonian "Epic of Creation," a poem which describes, in addition to the creation of the existing universe, the violent conflict between the powers of chaos and the creator whose victory alone made creation possible. In the Mesopotamian epic we assist at the councils of war of both parties; we are told of all their preparations and of the successive moods in which they watch the conflict develop. The issue seems in the balance until the very moment when battle is joined. In Egypt a similar situation is known, but it is treated very differently. The sun is celebrated as a victor, but not over chaos, which is seen as passive, awaiting the creator's initiative. The sun's enemy in Egypt is darkness, symbolized by the snake Apophis. Every night and at every dawn this antagonist is subdued. In the New Kingdom dull pictures without movement render the sun's victorious progress in his boat; the snake is slaughtered before the god (Figure 8). And in literature the theme is treated just as inadequately. The victory is mentioned but never described as an experience; it is entirely taken for granted. One hymn, which is more explicit than most, contains the following lines which render an address of the gods to the sun at its rising:

> Welcome, father of fathers and of all gods;
> Many-faced one, whose body one does not know;
> Who is warm of limb and shines in his sun disk;
> Who daily overthrows his enemies.
> The great uraeus at thy forehead punishes the evil dragon
> And cuts his spine;
> The flame destroys him;
> The heat devours him;
> Isis fights him;

Nephthys wounds him;
Thoth puts him to the sword and destroys him.
How beautiful is Re in his boat. . . .
Apophis fell before him,
His followers rejoice.[3]

Compared with others which have been preserved, this
description is exceptionally lively and detailed. Another
example may be taken from a papyrus which contains a
text to be recited at the temple service:

Thou risest, thou risest brilliantly;
Thou art victorious over thy enemies;
Thou causest the day-boat to sail past
And repellest the dragon of the storm at nighttime;
He cannot approach at the decisive moment;
Thou hast destroyed the power of the enemies;
The antagonists of Re are overthrown by the flame of terror.[4]

And so the hymn continues. It would be impossible to
treat a victory less as an achievement and more as a foregone conclusion. The thought that risks were entailed, that
an issue was at stake, is never allowed to arise. From
the first the tone is set; there is nowhere epic grandeur;
there is throughout a static splendor.

The absence of a progression of events in Egyptian
poetry does not mean that it is monotonous or ineffective,
but only that certain subjects which we consider suitable
for poetic treatment did not inspire the Egyptians. In the
preceding chapters we have quoted some remarkable
passages. I shall add here three from the sphere of religious
poetry.

The dead king Teti, alone in the darkness of the netherworld, appeals to his father, the sun-god Atum, who passes

[3] After Alexander Scharff, *Aegyptische Sonnenlieder* (Berlin, 1922), p. 33.
[4] *Ibid.*, p. 81.

nightly through the land of the dead. Teti offers some
services which he thinks he might be able to render the
god, but the allusions remain obscure. Nevertheless, the
passage seems to me to possess a curiously effective lyrical
unity:

> Father of Teti! Father of Teti in the darkness!
> Father of Teti! Atum in the darkness!
> Do fetch Teti to thy side!
> He will light the lamp for thee;
> He will protect thee, as Nun protected
> Those four goddesses on that day
> That they protected the throne.[5]

We quoted in the last chapter a text in which the dead
king was described as rising and setting with Atum (page
106). Sun and stars are described as being borne by the
sky-goddess Nut, the great mother, and the following text
is a prayer to her:

> Great One who became Heaven,
> Thou didst assume power, thou didst stir,
> Thou hast filled all places with thy beauty.
> The whole earth lies beneath thee.
> Thou hast taken possession of it.
> Thou enclosest the earth and all things [upon it] in thy arms.

And then follows the prayer for the sake of which all this
has been said: since Nut encloses all things in her arms
she also holds the dead king. Hence:

> Mayest thou put this king Pepi into thyself
> As an imperishable star.[6]

Yet another treatment of the king's ascent to heaven is
found in the following text, which shows an entirely different mood:

[5] Pyr. 605–6.   [6] Pyr. 782.

Flies who flies! He flies away from you, O men!
He is no longer upon earth, he is in the sky!
He rushes at the sky like a heron;
He has kissed the sky like a falcon;
He has leapt skyward like a grasshopper.[7]

All three quotations are from the Pyramid Texts and all three deal with the ascent of the dead king to heaven. I have chosen the examples within so narrow a range to emphasize the variety and force which Egyptian poetry sometimes possesses. Similar contrasts could be found in other periods and in connection with other subjects. The later hymns, and not only Akhenaten's famous sun-hymn, are quite often on a level with these older poems.

THE ABSENCE OF DRAMA

We cannot leave the field of religious poetry without mentioning drama. But it will be clear from what we have said already that in Egypt the conditions for its development were unfavorable. For in drama language is integrated with action and a change is shown to be a consequence of that action. Now it is true that within the Egyptian ritual the gods were sometimes represented by actors. An embalming priest wearing a jackal mask impersonated Anubis. In some texts the gods appear speaking and acting. The best preserved of these texts is the "Mystery Play of the Succession," which was performed when a new king came to the throne.[8]

But texts of this type do not represent a new art form; they are simply the "books" of rituals. They have been

[7] After Erman, *Literature*, p. 2.
[8] K. Sethe, *Dramatische Texte zu altaegyptischen Mysterienspielen* (Leipzig, 1928), discussed in my *Kingship and the Gods* (Chicago, 1948), Ch. 11.

called dramatic texts; they certainly are not drama. For their purpose is to translate actuality into the unchanging form of myth; for instance, when the death of a king causes a change in the person of the ruler, this historical event is presented in the ritual performance of the succession play as the perennial truth that Horus succeeds Osiris. The gods appear and speak once more the words they spoke "the first time." Thus the unavoidable change which takes place in the state is equated with the archetypal relationship between Osiris and his son and successor. The mythological situation is activated by the appearance of the gods who enunciate the traditional phrases. Hence that same tendency which led to a performance in which the gods appeared, and which thus received a semblance of drama, ran counter to the spirit of drama. For we do not find the representation of a change; on the contrary, a change which has taken place is reduced to a reaffirmation of an unchanging truth. If we judge, therefore, that the potentialities of the dramatic form which the Egyptians invented were not realized by them, we must also remember that they would not have valued its realization, since it would have meant making change the subject of art.

NARRATIVE VERSUS POETIC STYLE

The same reason which prevented the development of the drama and the epic myth explains the absence of the secular epic, the poem celebrating heroic deeds.[9] The Egyp-

[9] A possible exception is the description of the battle of Kadesh, although only the speeches of Ramses II and of some other personages seem to be poetry; it is not, therefore, strictly an epic, since the narrative is carried forward by prose in which the speeches, as poems, are embedded. In any case, this composition is as much at variance with Egyptian literary usage as are the reliefs depicting that battle, which represent a break with the

tian attitude towards such achievements as other peoples celebrated in epics can be well studied in the inscriptions of Tuthmosis III, a great soldier-king. He wished to place a record of his truly remarkable Syrian conquests in the Amon temple at Thebes. The form of this record is brutally matter-of-fact: mere excerpts from the diaries of the campaigns such as the following:

Year 23, first month of the third season . . . on the sixteenth day he arrived at the city of Yehem. . . .[10]

Another entry, a little more explicit, runs as follows:

Behold, the cultivable land was divided into fields, which the inspectors of the royal house (Life! Prosperity! Health!) calculated, in order to reap their harvest. Statement of the harvest which was brought to his majesty from the fields of Megiddo . . . 208,200 . . . fourfold heket measures of grain, besides that which was cut as forage by the army of his majesty . . .[11]

This is not merely prose, but the least artful form of prose. It is true that on closer inspection certain features of the annals are not a straight account of what happened but are remodeled according to the traditional view Egyptians took of the king; for instance, before entering a narrow pass there is a council of war; the generals hesitate to follow the impetuous decision of the king to send the army through, but Tuthmosis overrules them and is victorious. This has been proved to be an established literary convention in connection with Pharaoh.[12] But its inclu-

---

traditions of pictorial art. This will be further discussed in the book quoted at the end of the preceding chapter.
[10] J. H. Breasted, *Ancient Records of Egypt* (Chicago, 1907), II, § 419.
[11] *Ibid.*, § 437.
[12] A. de Buck, *Het Typische en het Individueele bij de Egyptenaren*. The latest translation of the description of the battle of Megiddo is by R. O. Faulkner, in *Journal of Egyptian Archaeology*, XXVIII (1942), 2–15.

sion in the businesslike annals merely shows once again that the ideal mattered more to the Egyptians than mere incidents of reality. And this is also shown by the very form of the annals. The diarylike summary of events is surely anything but a piece of literature. The facts were recorded; they did not deserve the beauty of literary expression.

We can be certain that this was the Egyptians' point of view because the achievements of Tuthmosis III were also sung by poets. And their composition was so much admired that two later kings—Seti I and Ramses III—copied it and adapted it for their own use. Now this poem contrasts in every respect with the annals; it has a most ingenious form, but it is practically bare of facts. It takes the form of an address to the victorious king by his father, Amon-Re. The introduction and the conclusion of the piece consist of flowery language of which it is hard to say whether it is prose or poetry. In any case, the god indicates the intimacy and the warmth of feeling which exist between himself and the king. For instance, Tuthmosis is addressed as follows:

> Thou comest to me, thou exultest seeing my beauty,
> O my son, my avenger, Menkheperre, living forever.
> I shine for love of thee,
> My heart is glad at thy beautiful comings into my temple;
> My two hands furnish thy limbs with protection . . .

And so forth! But after a number of these lines the poem assumes a very strict strophic form; this section consists of ten four-line stanzas, and the beginnings of all the first lines are the same and, similarly, the beginnings of all the third lines, throughout the poem. For instance (we must remember it is Amon who speaks):

I have come, causing thee to smite the princes of Zahi,
I have hurled them beneath thy feet among their high lands;
I have caused them to see Thy Majesty as a Lord of Radiance,
So that thou hast shone in their faces like my image.

I have come, causing thee to smite the Western Lands.
Keftiu and Cyprus are in terror.
I have caused them to see Thy Majesty as a young bull,
Firm of head, ready-horned, irresistible.

I have come, causing thee to smite those who are in the Isles;
Those who are in the midst of the sea hear thy roarings;
I have caused them to see Thy Majesty as a fierce-eyed lion,
Thou makest them corpses in their valleys.[13]

If we compare this poem with the annals, and remember that both compositions refer to the same events, it is clear that in Egypt the ingeniousness of the form of any piece of writing stands in inverse proportion to the factual information which it conveys. The annals tell us exactly the dates of the separate campaigns, the names of the places where the army camped, the amount of tribute paid by different vassals, and so on. But their form is artless, almost that of a calendar. The poem, on the other hand, is built up on a complex scheme of correspondences in line and image, but it confines itself to generalities. This is in keeping with a fact we have observed throughout the foregoing pages, namely, that the incidents of history, like all singular and isolated events, lacked real significance for the Egyptians. Facts can be recorded if that is desired, but not in a form which pretends to beauty or importance. On the contrary, the poet is inspired to his most ingenious com-

Ancient Egyptian Press Reset 8 Cal 23-9 DS July 18 *7
[13] After Breasted, *Ancient Records*, II, §§ 655–62. Here as elsewhere we have attempted to avoid quotations with allusions requiring comment. Hence we have combined, in the last stanza quoted, lines of two stanzas in the original, our purpose being merely to elucidate the poetical form of the composition.

positions by a contemplation of unchanging truth: Pharaoh is victorious, his father Amon-Re favors his campaigns. Some geographical names may be introduced (as we have observed) to add variety to the repeated statement of the theme. But the mention of the princes of Zahi, of the Lands of the West, or of Cyprus, stands on a par with the changing images for the king, who appears as Lord of Radiance, a young bull, or a fierce-eyed lion. The richness of the poetic texture is all that matters. We may even go further: It would seem (and I shall enlarge on this) that in Egypt poetic form could not be combined with exactitude of contents or the progression of a story; it would seem that either facts or poetry prevailed and that these states of mind were experienced as mutually exclusive by the Egyptians.

Let us, first of all, demonstrate that the texts of Tuthmosis III are typical examples; they faithfully reflect Egyptian usage. For instance, we find the same separation between facts and poetry in an inscription which is a thousand years older and which occurs in the tomb of Uni, an official of the Sixth Dynasty whom we have mentioned before (page 35 and following). He commanded a campaign in Palestine, and in his biography, engraved in his tomb, he first gives a straightforward description of the undertaking in prose, which contains all the facts. But then the text turns into a short hymn of two-lined stanzas, which convey no information whatsoever but repeat the theme with pleasing elegance:

> This army returned in safety
> After it had hacked up the land of the sand-dwellers.
>
> This army returned in safety
> After it had cut down its figs and vines.

This army returned in safety
After it had slain troops therein in many ten thousands.

And so forth.[14] It is clear, then, that Egyptian poetry refused to be burdened with the necessity of conveying information. It required a single mood and a single theme, and the richness and variety of its imagery seems to have formed the main source of aesthetic satisfaction to the ancients.

There is a curious feature in the form of these poems which deserves comment. You will have noticed that the compositions which are most accomplished in form start their stanzas with an identical line. We do not use that poetic form; we do know, however, stanzas ending with an identical line, the refrain. The difference between our usage and that of the Egyptians is most revealing. A refrain may be an epitome, in which case the stanzas appear as variations on a theme. But a poem with a refrain may amount to a statement that, whatever the circumstances which the stanzas describe, there is no change. In other words, such poems are based on an *expectation* of change. The Egyptian poems, starting each stanzas with the same line, exclude from the very first the possibility of change. They are, then, in exact agreement with the attitude of mind which we have throughout found to be characteristic of the Egyptians, namely, that only that which was changeless possessed significance.

The peculiarities of Egyptian poems dealing with what we should call epic subjects recur in philosophical poems. If we consider the "Dialogue of a Man Weary of Life with His Soul," we find, first of all, a discussion of the issue between the two. The issue is whether suicide is desirable

14 Breasted, *Ancient Records,* I, § 313. Textual marks omitted.

in the circumstances in which the man finds himself. We do not know (since the text is damaged) precisely what these circumstances were; it seems to me that the difficulty consisted in the fact that at the time no proper ritual burial could be assured. However, the issue itself does not concern us at present; we are interested in the literary form of the composition, and we note, then, that the actual discussion of the issue is rendered in prose. It consists of speeches by the man and by his soul, and these speeches are in prose. After the soul's second ripost the man recites four poems; all of these consist of three-line stanzas and within each poem all the stanzas start with the same line. I shall quote typical sections, mainly in the translation of Dr. J. A. Wilson.[15]

The first poem opens the man's address to his soul:

Behold, my name will reek through thee
  More than the stench of fishermen,
    More than the stagnant swamps where they have fished.

Behold, my name will reek through thee
  More than the stench of bird-droppings
    On summer days when the sky is hot.

There are eight of these stanzas. Then follow fifteen stanzas of the second poem:

    To whom can I speak today?
      One's fellows are evil;
        The friends of today do not love.

    To whom can I speak today?
      The gentle man has perished,
        The violent man has access to everybody.

[15] *The Intellectual Adventure of Ancient Man* (Chicago, 1946), pp. 102–3.

> To whom can I speak today?
>   Faces are invisible,
>   Each man looks down before his fellows.
>
> To whom can I speak today?
>   There are no righteous men,
>   The earth is surrendered to criminals.

The third poem has only six stanzas, and I quote three:

> Death stands before me today
>   Like the recovery of a sick man,
>   Like going outdoors again after being confined.
>
> Death stands before me today
>   Like the fragrance of myrrh,
>   Like sitting under a shade on a breezy day.
>
> Death stands before me today
>   As a man longs to see his house,
>   After he has spent many years held in captivity.

The last poem has only three stanzas; I shall quote two:

> Nay, but he who is yonder
>   Shall be a living god,
>   Inflicting punishment upon the doer of evil.
>
> Nay, but he who is yonder
>   Shall be a man of wisdom,
>   Not stopped from appealing to Re when he speaks.

The sequence of the four poems constitutes an argument but each poem in itself is but one isolated element of that argument, an element presented in a series of variations; the argument as such, moving from the premise to the conclusion, could apparently not be expressed in poetic form, so that the four poems follow one another without any connection between them. Yet together they present a logical line of thought. The man says to his soul: If I follow your advice I shall become an outcast ("My name will reek through thee"); moreover, present-day society is intolerable ("To whom can I speak today?"). Hence death is liberation, a way out of sorrow (third poem), and in the hereafter it will go well with me (fourth poem). We may assume that the elaboration of each step of the argument by the varied expression given to it in the stanzas of one poem made it sufficiently clear to the listeners how it was connected with the next step. In any case, the logical progression of the argument, the motivation of the sequence of the four poems, has not been made explicit. The composition ends with a short speech of the soul showing that the argument has been convincing, for it acquiesces in the action which the man is going to take. This speech is rendered again in prose.

THE SHORT STORY

The examples of Egyptian poetry which we have quoted included religious hymns, songs of victory, and—if the designation be accepted for our last example—philosophical secular poetry. The formal characteristics, and also the limitations and procedure, proved the same in all these categories, and the conclusions which we have drawn in the course of our discussion therefore reveal features which are truly characteristic. However, we must still consider prose as an art form. It is best known in the form of the short story, of which several highly accomplished examples are known. For our purpose, we need specimens which are preserved in their entirety so that their form, especially their composition, is clear. We have referred to these already (pages 46, 96). One, the story of Sinuhe, relates how its hero, on a campaign with the crown prince, overhears a messenger reporting the death of the king. The crown prince sets out at once and in secret for the capital to make sure of the succession, but Sinuhe knows of intrigues against him and possibly doubts the chances of success of his master; and the downfall of the crown prince would, of course, drag his supporters with it. The matter is left obscure because the text was written after the crown prince had, in fact, succeeded his father as Senusert I. The story merely describes how Sinuhe, panic-stricken, flees in the greatest confusion from the camp. He hides in the reeds, crosses a waterway in a boat without rudder; hides again and watches the sentries on a fortress wall at the frontier until the fall of night gives him a chance to cross over into the Sinai Desert. There he almost dies of thirst, is found by Bedaween, and becomes influential among them, after defeating an enemy of the tribe in single combat. He marries and settles, but retains contact with Egypt by eagerly receiving all messengers and travelers to and from the Nile Valley. In the end his old master, the king, summons him to return. His reception at court, with the queen and the princesses marveling at his barbaric appearance, is described in great detail. He is given a tomb (page 96 above) and thus reaches a happy old age.

We are inclined to read this truly entertaining story as a tale of adventure. But if we do that, we inevitably misjudge it. Peet, for instance, condemns it because the narrative is held up by a poem in praise of Senusert I, and by the insertion of the king's summons verbatim and Sinuhe's reply.[16] But these documents mark the turning

[16] T. E. Peet, A Comparative Study of the Literatures of Egypt, Palestine, and Mesopotamia (London, 1931), pp. 37 f.

point of the story. They show how a life unusually disturbed by strange but passing adventures is redeemed by reintegration in the established order of Egyptian society. The story of Sinuhe is not a tale of adventure; it deals with the values of life as they appeared to the Egyptians, not in the form of "teachings," but as exemplified by an exceptional career, a tale which shows what is lost by exile, and what can be retained, and even regained, by force of character. The sections which we are inclined to cut out, since they slow down the narrative, were for the Egyptians the highlights of the document. Sinuhe's adventures, on the other hand, are clearly shown to be without ultimate significance by the fact that they make no difference at all. At the end of the story the hero is back at his starting point, established as a favored servant of Senusert I. All he has acquired in Asia he has left behind, even his family. In the end he is shown to have gained nothing but this: The consequences of his impulsive act, which made him break away from the service of his royal master, are obliterated.

The correctness of this interpretation is shown by another tale which is also almost completely preserved, the "Eloquent Peasant." It was as popular as the story of Sinuhe and hence is preserved in several copies. I quote, in Dr. Gardiner's translation, the beginning as an example of the Egyptian's accomplishment as a narrator: [17]

There was once a man whose name was Khunanup, a peasant of the Sekhet Hmuet; and he had a wife whose name was Marye. And this peasant said to her his wife: "Behold I am going

[17] After Gardiner, in *Journal of Egyptian Archaeology*, IX (1923), 7 ff. In view of our purpose, we have omitted diacritical marks, indications of uncertainties in the reading, and other notes which would distract the reader.

down into Egypt to bring food thence for my children. Go now, measure out for me the corn which is in the barn, the remainder of last harvest's corn." Then he measured out to her six gallons of corn.

And this peasant said to his wife: "Behold, there are left over twenty gallons of corn to be food for thee and thy children; but make thou for me these six gallons of corn into bread and beer for every day in which I shall be travelling."

So this peasant went down into Egypt, after that he had loaded his asses with rushes, . . . natron, salt, . . . leopard skins, wolf furs, bamboo, . . . And this peasant departed southward toward Nenesu and arrived in the vicinity of Per-fiofi to the north of Medene; and he found a man standing on the river-bank named Thothnakht, the son of a man whose name was Isry, a vassal of the high steward Rensi, the son of Meru.

And this Thothnakht said, when he saw asses belonging to this peasant which were desirable in his heart: "Would that I had some potent idol that I might steal away the belongings of this peasant withal!" Now the house of this Thothnakht was on the riverside path, which was narrow and not broad, equal to the breadth of a loincloth; and the one side of it was under water, and the other under corn.

And this Thothnakht said to his servant: "Go, bring me a cloth from my house." And it was brought to him straightway. Then he stretched it over the riverside path, so that its fringe rested on the water and its hem on the corn. Then came this peasant along the public road.

And this Thothnakht said: "Have a care, peasant; wouldst tread on my garments?"

And this peasant said: "I will do thy pleasure; my course is a good one." So he went up higher.

And this Thothnakht said: "Shalt thou have my corn for a path?"

And this peasant said: "My course is a good one. The bank is high and our only course is under corn; and still thou cumberest our way with thy garments. Wilt thou then not let us pass along the road?"

Thereupon one of the asses filled its mouth with a wisp of corn. And this Thothnakht said: "Behold, I will take away thy ass, peasant, because it is eating my corn. Behold, it shall toil because of its offence."

And this peasant said: "My course is a good one. Only one [18] has been hurt. I brought my donkey on account of its endurance, thou takest it away for the filling of its mouth with a wisp of corn. Nay, but I know the lord of this domain. It belongs to the high steward Rensi, the son of Meru. It is he who restrains every robber throughout the entire land; and shall I then be robbed in his own domain?"

And this Thothnakht said: "Is this the proverb which people say: The poor man's name is not pronounced save for his master's sake? It is I who speak to thee, and it is the high steward whom thou callest to mind!"

Then he took up a rod of green tamarisk against him and belaboured all his limbs therewith; seized his asses and drove them into his domain.

Thereupon this peasant fell a-weeping very bitterly for the pain of that which was done to him. And this Thothnakht said: "Lift not up thy voice, peasant. Behold, thou art bound for the abode of the Lord of Silence!" [19]

And this peasant said: "Thou beatest me, thou stealest away my goods; and then takest thou the complaint from my mouth! Thou Lord of Silence, give me back my chattels, so that I may cease to cry out thy disturbance!"

And this peasant tarried for ten long spaces over ten days making petition to this Thothnakht, but he paid no heed to it. So this peasant departed to Nenesu in order to make petition to the high steward Rensi, the son of Meru, and found him as he was coming forth from the door of his house to go down into his barge belonging to the judgment hall.[20]

And this peasant said: "Would that I might be permitted to

[18] *Scil.* wisp of corn.
[19] The land of the dead; see p. 108 above.
[20] Rensi was just going to a session of the court and was using the official barge.

rejoice thy heart with this narration. Were it possible that a servant of thy choice might come to me, so that he might bear tidings from me to thee concerning it?"

So the high steward Rensi, the son of Meru, caused a servant of his choice to go in front of him in order that he might bring tidings from this peasant concerning this matter in its every aspect.[21] Then the high steward Rensi, the son of Meru, laid an information against this Thothnakht before the magistrates who were with him.

And they said to him: "Probably it is some peasant of his who has come to someone else beside him. Behold, that is what they use to do to peasants of theirs who have come to others beside themselves. Is it a case for one's punishing this Thothnakht on account of a trifle of natron and a trifle of salt? Let him be commanded to replace it, so that he may replace it."

But the high steward Rensi, the son of Meru, held his peace and answered not these magistrates,[22] neither did he answer this peasant.

The peasant then makes a petition to the high steward in such unusually beautiful language that Rensi reports it to the king. Pharaoh commands that the peasant's case shall not be decided for a while so that he shall be obliged to make further petitions, and these must be put down in writing. Meanwhile Rensi takes care of the peasant's family, although the peasant does not know it. There follow eight petitions, and these form the bulk of our text. Consequently they must be the cause of its popularity in Egypt. Modern critics, however, condemn them one and all as monotonous and artificial. They consist of passages like the following:

Is it not wrong, a balance which tilts, a plummet which deflects, a straightforward man who is become a shirker? Behold,

---

[21] The peasant and the servant go on ahead of Rensi by land, so that Rensi is able at once to lay the matter before his colleagues on the bench.
[22] For the implications of this silence see p. 66 above and p. 70, n. 12.

justice (Maat) escapes (?) from beneath thee, being expelled from its place . . .[23]

The poor man's possessions are breath to him, and one who takes them away stoppeth up his nose. Thou wast appointed to hear pleas, to decide between suitors, to repress the brigand; and behold, what thou dost is to support the thief. One puts faith in thee, and thou art become a transgressor. Thou wast set for a dam unto the poor man, take heed lest he drown; behold, thou art a swift current to him.[24]

We do not relish page after page of such sayings but they resemble the "teachings" which we discussed in the third chapter. They also remind us of the peculiarities of Egyptian poetry. In artistic prose, too, the progression of a story or an argument was not considered the most important element of a work of literature. Here, as in the poems, we find a single mood and a single subject, presented with rich variation. And the subjects considered worthy of such artful and laborious treatment are, in prose as in poetry, the unchanging values of life. If we are to understand the Egyptian and understand the works he left us, we must agree with his basic conviction that the touchstone of significance is permanence.

ARCHITECTURAL FORMS

The same conviction determined the character of Egyptian art. We shall demonstrate this here in the province of architecture. The permanence of Egyptian monuments is proverbial with us, and it is even true to say that the introduction of stone architecture, an Egyptian invention of far-reaching importance, was due to the wish to ensure the permanence of buildings. The earliest stone structure,

[23] Gardiner, in *Journal of Egyptian Archaeology*, IX (1923), 11, ll. 96–98.
[24] *Ibid.*, 16, ll. 234–37.

Djoser's funerary complex at Saqqara, imitated with painful precision traditional structures of reed and wood from
which it was meant to differ in durability alone. Egyptian
stone architecture thus possessed a paradoxical character
from the first. Soon after its invention, under the Fourth
Dynasty, at least in the necropolis at Gizeh, its peculiar
potentialities were realized. The unadorned oblong tombs
surrounding the king's pyramid, the bare monolithic pillars
of red granite placed on an alabaster floor in the funerary
temples (Figure 27), all these achieved effects for which
the distinctive qualities of stone—its massiveness, texture,
and color—were exclusively responsible. But immediately
afterwards, in the Fifth Dynasty, the Egyptians broke
away from this austere style. They returned to the use
of relief and invented ornamental columns which have remained characteristic of Egyptian architecture ever since.
They utilized plant forms. A bundle of lotus or papyrus
flowers (Figure 23) or, more rarely, a palm tree (Figure
28) were translated into architectural supports. At this
time there is no question of imitation. There is no prototype of the papyrus column in primitive reed architecture;
the Fifth Dynasty created new and purely architectural
forms. The columns have a base, a shaft, a capital, and an
abacus to carry the architrave. Natural forms are only used
to the extent that they can be made to serve architectural
ends: the triangular section of the papyrus column supplies the sharp ribbing of the shaft. The rope which holds
the bundle together becomes a border separating shaft
and capital. The sheaths from which the stalks sprout are
made into a pattern which sets off the base of the shaft
from the column base, and in a like manner the bracts of
the flowers mark the lower edge of the capital. If we re-

call the appearance of the papyrus plant in nature (Figure 24) we shall admit that the column represents no mean artistic creation.

Yet, for all their logical articulation, the plant columns remain problematical, at least to modern students of art. We question whether renderings of tender buds and flowers should be made to carry tons of stone. But the Egyptians, even on the rare occasions when they used the palm tree as the prototype for their columns (Figure 28), supported the architrave, not on the stem, but on the stylized crown of palm fronds; they evidently did not share our appreciation of functional appropriateness. It is, however, astonishing that they were not disturbed by another aspect of the plant column. Flowering plants almost everywhere call forth the very thought of transitoriness which the Egyptians attempted to banish. We must conclude that lotus and papyrus possessed for them associations of a different order which prevented the realization of the perishable nature of the plants from coming to the fore. The clue to an understanding of the plant columns lies in their disposition in buildings.

The arrangement of columns in Egyptian buildings diverge noticeably from our own usage. It is true that columns were sometimes used with an effect which we too admire, in private houses, rock tombs, and temple porticoes; we even find in the applied arts a charming use of diminutive plant columns, for instance as mirror handles. But if we must single out the use of the plant column which is most characteristic of Egypt, we think of its massed occurrence in the temples of the second and first millenniums B.C. (Figure 26). We are oppressed by the lack of space between these bulky supports which crowd the hypostyle

halls and colonnades in a manner not adequately explained
by the limited length of the stone architraves. For art as
vital as that of ancient Egypt is not subject to the limitations of materials, but, on the contrary, chooses materials
which enable it the fullest scope of expression. We must
grant that the Egyptians did not find the massing of columns objectionable, and even that this feature of their
temples may have had a positive value for them. We find,
then, that in the use of their very original columns no less
than in their conception, the Egyptians were guided by
tendencies which are strange to us.

We may understand these tendencies best by considering their effect on temple planning (Figure 29). The
basic plan of an Egyptian temple is logical and compre-
hensible. The Holy of Holies was a small dark room in the
central axis of the temple towards the back. It thus appears as at the end of a long road which passed through
the forecourts and narrowed through porticos and halls
until the hidden shrine was reached. This road also
mounted, steeply in the case of the pyramid temples and
the rock temples, less noticeably in other cases. But at
every door we find a few steps or a ramp to mark the rise.
For the Holy of Holies was ideally conceived as the
primeval hill, the first land to arise from the waters of
chaos on the day of creation.[25] Since all that exists had
gone forth from this spot, it was a center of immeasurable
potency well suited for the manifestation of a divinity.

The conception of the shrine as the primeval hill is expressed in the names of most of Egypt's famous sanctuaries. It also explains the peculiarities of Egyptian temple

[25] A. de Buck, *De egyptische Voorstellingen betreffende den Oerheuvel*
(Leiden, 1922).

architecture, in the first place the use of plant columns. The waters of chaos and the primeval hill formed a sort of landscape of "the first time" which played as great a part in the religious imagination of the Egyptians as did the Judaean hills with the Garden of Gethsemane and the Mount of Golgotha in that of Christians. The Egyptian religious landscape was a vast expanse of marsh (Figure 24). It is almost ubiquitous in religious literature. It is present in the belief in an afterlife as the Field of Rushes (page 110 and following). It is the scene in which the ancient image of the mother-goddess Hathor, the wild cow, manifests herself by parting the reeds with her head (Figure 25). It affects the images of the sun-god in many ways; he was for instance thought to have appeared as a child sitting in the flower of a lotus; he was thought to cross the heavens in floats made of reeds; as Amon-Re he was sometimes thought to have emerged from an egg which rested on the primeval hill, and to have flown in the form of a goose over the waters, his honking the first sound ever made.

Lotus and papyrus were essential constituents of this unchanging significant "landscape of the first time." It was not their perishable nature that impressed the Egyptians; on the contrary, the decay of the individual plants was a meaningless incident in comparison with the perennial presence of the species in the scenery from which the universe had gone forth, and which was a reality ever-present in man's thought through the religious imagery which we have mentioned. In the stone columns of the temples the perishable nature of the plants had been overcome but their true significance preserved. These columns banned the religious landscape to the site of the temple, their massed disposition intensifying the effect. For the temple, in Egypt, was a place of power. The gods were immanent in nature, and hence difficult to localize. The temple cast a spell, as it were, on a given spot where divinities might be approached. This explains the confusion which the main sanctuaries of Egypt, at Karnak (Figure 30) and Luxor, present—a confusion which remains impossible to understand if we approach them as works of architecture. We have seen that the basic plan of the Egyptian temple was simple and logical. But the sanctuaries which enjoyed the greatest prestige during the New Kingdom (and of those of the Old and Middle Kingdoms we know very little) are disorderly conglomerates; the road from entrance to Holy of Holies was lengthened by the addition of new courts and pylons in successive reigns, or even during the reign of the founder. Subordinate shrines were built at the sides or included within the sacred area when it was enlarged. We miss in this unrestricted extension of an architectural whole a sense of proportion, a feeling for inherent harmony which put definite limits to the additions which an original layout is able to accommodate. But the royal building inscriptions indicate that the Egyptians felt each addition to be not only a credit to the builder, but of value to the shrine. For if the supreme power of Amon was expressed by the superlative size of the Karnak temple, the temple gained power too; the accumulated efforts of generations intensified the spell which made the elusive deity, who was manifest in wind and light (page 26 and following), easy of approach at Karnak.

There was, however, an alternative to the confusion which a temple complex like Karnak displays. If size and mass represent potency, it is possible to satisfy the craving for the gigantic without creating disorder. This can be done if one compels the mass to assume a clear abstract form. This solution was adopted when the kings of the Old Kingdom constructed their tombs in the form of the pyramid (Figure 31). The pyramid, like the shrine on its elevation, symbolized the primeval hill. But no description and no picture can do justice to these monuments. Their actual size is an important element in the overwhelming impression which they create when one succeeds in contemplating them from the desert side, distant from the distractions through which one is unfortunately compelled to approach them. We must remember that they were originally cased from tip to base with smooth stones of which even the joints were next to invisible. Thus these symbols of the place where all life had originated were free from every particularization which would call up the thought of an alternative—and hence of transcience. They are beyond change.

The pyramids cannot be compared with any other type of structure. They are completely inaccessible. The temples belonging to them lie at their base, but the pyramid itself, once the royal body had been interred, was closed hermetically and every trace of the mouth of the shaft was obliterated. They well illustrate, therefore, at the end of our considerations, the theme which recurred throughout, to wit, that Egyptian accomplishments are apt to assume in our eyes a paradoxical character. The greatest triumphs of the inventors of stone architecture are structures which hardly enter into our architectural categories. But they do express, with unanswerable finality, the ancient Egyptian's conviction that his universe was a world without change.

1. ISIS, TOMB OF HAREMHAB, THEBES

2. ANUBIS, TOMB OF HAREMHAB, THEBES

3. THOTH AS BABOON, WITH A SCRIBE
TELL EL AMARNA

4. THOTH AS IBIS, WITH TWO
BABOONS AND THE GODDESS MAAT
HILDESHEIM

5. THOTH BEFORE KING SETI I, ABYDOS
Calverley, Temple of King Sethos I, *Vol. III*, Pl. *39*

6. SETI I BEFORE THE GODDESS HEQT, ABYDOS
Calverley, Temple of King Sethos I, *Vol. III*, Pl. *14*

7. KHAFRA AND THE HORUS-FALCON, CAIRO
Photo Marburg

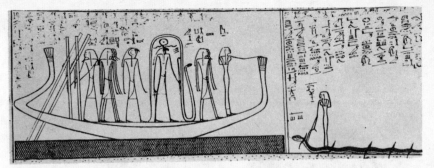

8. DESTRUCTION OF THE SERPENT BEFORE THE SUN BOAT, TOMB OF SETI I, THEBES
Courtesy Metropolitan Museum of Art, New York

9. THE COW OF HEAVEN, TOMB OF SETI I, THEBES
Journal of Egyptian Archaeology, XXVIII (1942), Pl. IV

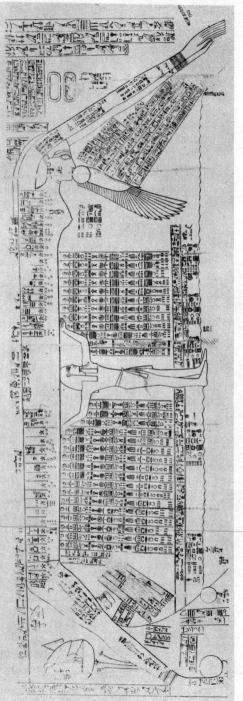

10. NUT AND THE HEAVENS, CENOTAPH OF SETI I, ABYDOS
Courtesy Egypt Exploration Society

11. HATHOR CAPITAL FROM BUBASTIS
Courtesy Museum of Fine Arts, Boston

12. HATHOR PROTECTING
KING PSAMMETICHOS, CAIRO

13. TAURT, CAIRO

14. HATHOR
*Collection of the New York Historical
Society in the Brooklyn Museum*

15. TUTHMOSIS III VICTORIOUS OVER SYRIANS, KARNAK

16. RAMSES III VICTORIOUS OVER LIBYANS, MEDINET HABU
Courtesy Oriental Institute, University of Chicago

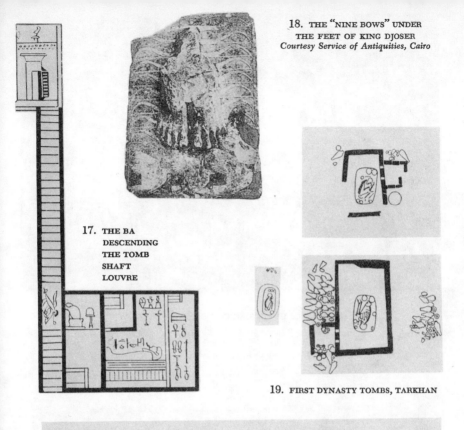

18. THE "NINE BOWS" UNDER
THE FEET OF KING DJOSER
Courtesy Service of Antiquities, Cairo

17. THE BA
DESCENDING
THE TOMB
SHAFT
LOUVRE

19. FIRST DYNASTY TOMBS, TARKHAN

20. BA NEAR MUMMY, COPENHAGEN
Courtesy Ny Carlsberg Glyptothek

21. FALSE DOOR IN TOMB CHAPEL OF TI

22. FALSE DOOR IN TOMB CHAPEL OF MERERUKA
Courtesy Oriental Institute, University of Chicago

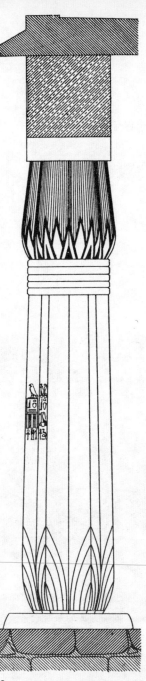

23. PAPYRUS COLUMN FROM THE
FUNERARY TEMPLE OF NEUSERRE
ABUSIR

24. PAPYRUS MARSH ON THE UPPER NILE
Courtesy American Museum of Natural History, New York

25. HATHOR AMONG THE REEDS
FROM DEIR EL BAHRI, CAIRO

26. TEMPLE OF KHONSU, KARNAK

27. TEMPLE OF KHAFRA, GIZEH

28. MODEL OF TEMPLE OF SAHURE, ABUSIR
Courtesy Oriental Institute, University of Chicago

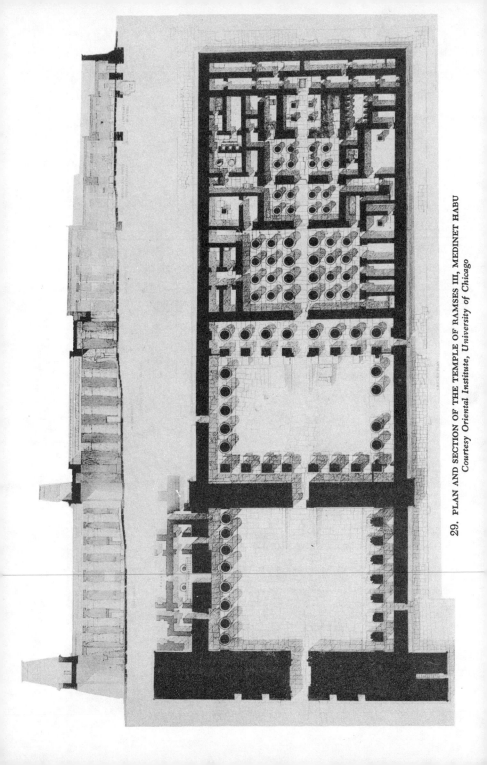

29. PLAN AND SECTION OF THE TEMPLE OF RAMSES III, MEDINET HABU

Courtesy Oriental Institute, University of Chicago

30. AIR VIEW OF KARNAK
Photo Kofler

31. AIR VIEW OF THE PYRAMIDS AT GIZEH
Courtesy Mr. J. H. Breasted, Jr.

Index

Abydos, cemeteries at, 105

Air, Shu as, 19, 52; a cosmic power, 14; creative, 22; combined significance of sun and, 26

Akh, defined, 63; transfigured spirits of the dead, 96, 100, 106

Akhenaten, monotheistic cult, 3, 25, 54, 135

Amenemope, 69; teachings, excerpts, 66 f., 72, 73, 75, 80

Amenhotep III, 55

Amon, 78; manifest in wind and breath, 22; restoration of cult, 54; Karnak temple, 155

Amon-Re, 138, 140; rise of, as supreme god, 22; immanent in nature, 23; texts describing all-pervading power, 26, 27; depiction, 154; see also Re

Ani, Papyrus of, 35

Animals, role in religion, 8-14; worship in Africa and America, 9; mummified, 9; connection between gods and, 9 ff., 14; hybrid forms, 10 ff., 15; awe felt before all animal life, 12; existence in unchanging species, 13, 88; interpretation of the otherness of, 13 f.; association with great cosmic gods, 14 f.; see also names of species, e.g., Cow; Snake; etc.

Anubis, manifestations, 10 f., 135

Apis bull, 10

Apophis, snake, 18, 132

Architecture, forms, 150-56; potentialities of stone, 151; relief and ornamental columns, 151 ff.; temple plan, 153 ff.; pyramids, 154

Art, hybrid or transitional forms, common in, 11 f.; different conceptions combined in, 19; prevalence of typical over individual features in literary and plastic monuments of king, 46-49; tomb sculptures, reliefs, and paintings, 47-49, 56, 93, 94, 97, 122; paradoxes in field of, 124 f.; permanence as touchstone of significance, demonstrated in the province of architecture, 150-56

Asiatics, conquest by, 84

Aten cult, 25; see Monotheism

Attunement to society and nature, success as, 65-72

Atum, 52, 133, 134; dialogue between Osiris and, 119 f.

Ba, meaning, 96; dead manifest as, 97, 99, 100

Ba-bird, 12n, 97, 98

Baboon, 10, 79

Babylonians, 97; "Epic of Creation," 132

Battle reliefs, 48, 56

Beetle, 19

Bible, 76, 77, 81; the Gospels, 3, 154; Old Testament, 3, 27, 51, 61, 132; Jahweh in, 26, 27, 51; concept of evil, 73; ideal of perfection, 74

Biographies, see Funerary literature; Teachings

Birdlike apparitions of the dead, 97 f.

Book of Gates, 117

"Book of the Dead," 92, 100, 111, 117, 120; excerpt, 52

Books, see Teachings

Nubia, expeditions to, 38, 39

Nun, primeval ocean, 52, 112, 114, 134

Nut, sky-goddess, 17, 52, 112; depiction, 15; prayer to, 134

Ocean, primeval, 52, 114

Officials, *see* Bureaucracy

Old Testament, *see* Bible

Order, divine: justice as, 54; *see also* Justice; Maat

Orion, star, 111, 113

Osiris, 28, 88, 117; myth of Horus, Isis, and, 7, 102 ff., 126-31, 136; as earth and its recurrent life, 103, 105; identification of the dead with, 103 ff.; responsibility of son for, 104*n*; "religion of," 107; dialogue between Atum and, 119 f.; hymn to, 130

Otto, Rudolf, 13

Paintings, *see* Art

Palm tree as prototype for column, 151, 152

Papyrus, architectural ornament, 151, 154

Papyrus Chester Beatty, 128, 130

Paradoxes, in religion: reason for and meaning of, 3 ff.; in fields of literature and art, 124-26

Passionate man, 65-76 *passim*

Peak, the, 77, 78

Peet, T. E., 145

People, the: political status and economic services, 36-46; extent of personal freedom, 42, 58; *see also* Human life

Pepi II, victory over Libyans, 48, 55; in the cosmic circuit, 112-14, 134

Pepinakht, funerary text, 45; excerpt, 82

Permanence, touchstone of significance, 49-53; universe comprehended as essentially static, 49, 50; significance of the creation story, 50 ff.; Maat, the order upon

which society forever founded, 54 ff.; uniformity of "teachings" in earlier and later texts, 59; ideals of progress and change excluded by belief in static universe, 64; significance of tradition, 80-87; of buildings, 150; pyramids as symbols, 156; *see also* Change

Pharaoh, *see* Kingship and king

Phoenix, 97

Plant columns, 151 f., 154

Plutarch, account of Osiris myth, 126 ff.

Poetry, ideals and feelings expressed: harpers' song, excerpt, 83; forms, 125 f., 144; myths not told in religions, 126; references to mythological events, 129 f., 132-35; variety and force, 135; narrative vs. poetic style, 136-44; difference between Egyptian and our usage, 141; *see also* Hymns

Political catastrophe, nature and effects of, 84 ff.

Political organization, 33-36, 40, 42-46, 55

Polytheism, 4

Power, divine: of king, 6 (*see also* Kingship); immanence, 19

Pragmatic misinterpretation of the "teachings," 62-65

Pride, 68 ff.

Procreation, 20, 52

Progress and other changes, ideals of: excluded by belief in static universe, 64

Prose vs. poetic style, 136-44; short story, 144-50

Ptah, earth-god, 77; relation between Apis bull and, 10; creative power, 20, 23, 24, 51

"Ptahhotep, Teachings of," excerpts, 61-74 *passim*

Pyramid architecture, 156

Pyramid Texts, 54, 55, 90, 100, 106, 111, 112, 113, 126, 135

harper ✦ torchbooks

American Studies: General

HENRY ADAMS Degradation of the Democratic Dogma. ‡ *Introduction by Charles Hirschfeld.* TB/1450

LOUIS D. BRANDEIS: Other People's Money, *and How the Bankers Use It. Ed. with Intro, by Richard M. Abrams* TB/3081

HENRY STEELE COMMAGER, Ed.: The Struggle for Racial Equality TB/1300

CARL N. DEGLER: Out of Our Past: *The Forces that Shaped Modern America* CN/2

CARL N. DEGLER, Ed.: Pivotal Interpretations of American History
Vol. I TB/1240; Vol. II TB/1241

A. S. EISENSTADT, Ed.: The Craft of American History: *Selected Essays*
Vol. I TB/1255; Vol. II TB/1256

LAWRENCE H. FUCHS, Ed.: American Ethnic Politics TB/1368

MARCUS LEE HANSEN: The Atlantic Migration: 1607-1860. *Edited by Arthur M. Schlesinger. Introduction by Oscar Handlin* TB/1052

MARCUS LEE HANSEN: The Immigrant in American History. *Edited with a Foreword by Arthur M. Schlesinger* TB/1120

ROBERT L. HEILBRONER: The Limits of American Capitalism TB/1305·

JOHN HIGHAM, Ed.: The Reconstruction of American History TB/1068

ROBERT H. JACKSON: The Supreme Court in the American System of Government TB/1106

JOHN F. KENNEDY: A Nation of Immigrants. *Illus. Revised and Enlarged. Introduction by Robert F. Kennedy* TB/1118

LEONARD W. LEVY, Ed.: American Constitutional Law: *Historical Essays* TB/1285

LEONARD W. LEVY, Ed.: Judicial Review and the Supreme Court TB/1296

LEONARD W. LEVY: The Law of the Commonwealth and Chief Justice Shaw: *The Evolution of American Law, 1830-1860* TB/1309

GORDON K. LEWIS: Puerto Rico: *Freedom and Power in the Caribbean. Abridged edition* TB/1371

GUNNAR MYRDAL: An American Dilemma: *The Negro Problem and Modern Democracy. Introduction by the Author.*
Vol. I TB/1443; Vol. II TB/1444

GILBERT OSOFSKY, Ed.: The Burden of Race: *A Documentary History of Negro-White Relations in America* TB/1405

ARNOLD ROSE: The Negro in America: *The Condensed Version of Gunnar Myrdal's An American Dilemma. Second Edition* TB/3048

JOHN E. SMITH: Themes in American Philosophy: *Purpose, Experience and Community* TB/1466

WILLIAM R. TAYLOR: Cavalier and Yankee: *The Old South and American National Character* TB/1474

American Studies: Colonial

BERNARD BAILYN: The New England Merchants in the Seventeenth Century TB/1149

ROBERT E. BROWN: Middle-Class Democracy and Revolution in Massachusetts, 1691-1780. *New Introduction by Author* TB/1413

JOSEPH CHARLES: The Origins of the American Party System TB/1049

WESLEY FRANK CRAVEN: The Colonies in Transition: 1660-1712† TB/3084

CHARLES GIBSON: Spain in America † TB/3077

CHARLES GIBSON, Ed.: The Spanish Tradition in America + HR/1351

LAWRENCE HENRY GIPSON: The Coming of the Revolution: 1763-1775. † *Illus.* TB/3007

JACK P. · GREENE, Ed.: Great Britain and the American Colonies: 1606-1763. + *Introduction by the Author* HR/1477

AUBREY C. LAND, Ed.: Bases of the Plantation Society + HR/1429

PERRY MILLER: Errand Into the Wilderness TB/1139

PERRY MILLER & T. H. JOHNSON, Ed.: The Puritans: *A Sourcebook of Their Writings*
Vol. I TB/1093; Vol. II TB/1094

EDMUND S. MORGAN: The Puritan Family: *Religion and Domestic Relations in Seventeenth Century New England* TB/1227

WALLACE NOTESTEIN: The English People on the Eve of Colonization: 1603-1630. † *Illus.* TB/3006

LOUIS B. WRIGHT: The Cultural Life of the American Colonies: 1607-1763. † *Illus.* TB/3005

YVES F. ZOLTVANY, Ed.: The French Tradition in America + HR/1425

American Studies: The Revolution to 1860

JOHN R. ALDEN: The American Revolution: 1775-1783. † *Illus.* TB/3011

† The New American Nation Series, edited by Henry Steele Commager and Richard B. Morris.
‡ American Perspectives series, edited by Bernard Wishy and William E. Leuchtenburg.
a History of Europe series, edited by J. H. Plumb.
§ The Library of Religion and Culture, edited by Benjamin Nelson.
‖ Researches in the Social, Cultural, and Behavioral Sciences, edited by Benjamin Nelson.
Σ Harper Modern Science Series, edited by James A. Newman.
° Not for sale in Canada.
+ Documentary History of the United States series, edited by Richard B. Morris.
# Documentary History of Western Civilization series, edited by Eugene C. Black and Leonard W. Levy.
ᴧ The Economic History of the United States series, edited by Henry David et al.
¶ European Perspectives series, edited by Eugene C. Black.
** Contemporary Essays series, edited by Leonard W. Levy.
* The Stratum Series, edited by John Hale.

RAY A. BILLINGTON: The Far Western Frontier: 1830-1860. † *Illus.* TB/3012
STUART BRUCHEY: The Roots of American Economic Growth, 1607-1861: *An Essay in Social Causation. New Introduction by the Author.* TB/1350
WHITNEY R. CROSS: The Burned-Over District: *The Social and Intellectual History of Enthusiastic Religion in Western New York, 1800-1850* TB/1242
NOBLE E. CUNNINGHAM, JR., Ed.: The Early Republic, 1789-1828 + HR/1394
GEORGE DANGERFIELD: The Awakening of American Nationalism, 1815-1828. † *Illus.* TB/3061
CLEMENT EATON: The Freedom-of-Thought Struggle in the Old South. *Revised and Enlarged. Illus.* TB/1150
CLEMENT EATON: The Growth of Southern Civilization, 1790-1860. † *Illus.* TB/3040
ROBERT H. FERRELL, Ed.: Foundations of American Diplomacy, 1775-1872 + HR/1393
LOUIS FILLER: The Crusade against Slavery: 1830-1860. † *Illus.* TB/3029
DAVID H. FISCHER: The Revolution of American Conservatism: *The Federalist Party in the Era of Jeffersonian Democracy* TB/1449
WILLIM W. FREEHLING: Prelude to Civil War: *The Nullification Controversy in South Carolina, 1816-1836* TB/1359
PAUL W. GATES: The Farmer's Age: *Agriculture, 1815-1860* △ TB/1398
THOMAS JEFFERSON: Notes on the State of Virginia. ‡ *Edited by Thomas P. Abernethy* TB/3052
FORREST MCDONALD, Ed.: Confederation and Constitution, 1781-1789 + HR/1396
BERNARD MAYO: Myths and Men: *Patrick Henry, George Washington, Thomas Jefferson* TB/1108
JOHN C. MILLER: Alexander Hamilton and the Growth of the New Nation TB/3057
JOHN C. MILLER: The Federalist Era: 1789-1801. † *Illus.* TB/3027
RICHARD B. MORRIS, Ed.: Alexander Hamilton and the Founding of the Nation. *New Introduction by the Editor* TB/1448
RICHARD B. MORRIS: The American Revolution Reconsidered TB/1363
CURTIS P. NETTELS: The Emergence of a National Economy, 1775-1815 △ TB/1438
DOUGLASS C. NORTH & ROBERT PAUL THOMAS, Eds.: *The Growth of the American Economy to 1860* + HR/1352
R. B. NYE: The Cultural Life of the New Nation: 1776-1830. † *Illus.* TB/3026
GILBERT OSOFSKY, Ed.: Puttin' On Ole Massa: *The Slave Narratives of Henry Bibb, William Wells Brown, and Solomon Northup* ‡ TB/1432
JAMES PARTON: The Presidency of Andrew Jackson. *From Volume III of the* Life of Andrew Jackson. *Ed. with Intro. by Robert V. Remini* TB/3080
FRANCIS S. PHILBRICK: The Rise of the West, 1754-1830. † *Illus.* TB/3067
MARSHALL SMELSER: The Democratic Republic, 1801-1815 † TB/1406
JACK M. SOSIN, Ed.: The Opening of the West + HR/1424
GEORGE ROGERS TAYLOR: The Transportation Revolution, 1815-1860 △ TB/1347
A. F. TYLER: Freedom's Ferment: *Phases of American Social History from the Revolution to the Outbreak of the Civil War. Illus.* TB/1074
GLYNDON G. VAN DEUSEN: The Jacksonian Era: 1828-1848. † *Illus.* TB/3028

LOUIS B. WRIGHT: Culture on the Moving Frontier TB/1053

American Studies: The Civil War to 1900

W. R. BROCK: An American Crisis: *Congress and Reconstruction, 1865-67* ° TB/1283
T. C. COCHRAN & WILLIAM MILLER: The Age of Enterprise: *A Social History of Industrial America* TB/1054
W. A. DUNNING: Reconstruction, Political and Economic: 1865-1877 TB/1073
HAROLD U. FAULKNER: Politics, Reform and Expansion: 1890-1900. † *Illus.* TB/3020
GEORGE M. FREDRICKSON: The Inner Civil War: *Northern Intellectuals and the Crisis of the Union* TB/1358
JOHN A. GARRATY: The New Commonwealth, 1877-1890 † TB/1410
JOHN A. GARRATY, Ed.: The Transformation of American Society, 1870-1890 + HR/1395
HELEN HUNT JACKSON: A Century of Dishonor: *The Early Crusade for Indian Reform.* † *Edited by Andrew F. Rolle* TB/3063
WILLIAM G. MCLOUGHLIN, Ed.: The American Evangelicals, 1800-1900: An Anthology ‡ TB/1382
ARNOLD M. PAUL: Conservative Crisis and the Rule of Law: *Attitudes of Bar and Bench, 1887-1895. New Introduction by Author* TB/1415
JAMES S. PIKE: The Prostrate State: *South Carolina under Negro Government.* ‡ *Intro. by Robert F. Durden* TB/3085
WHITELAW REID: After the War: *A Tour of the Southern States, 1865-1866.* ‡ *Edited by C. Vann Woodward* TB/3066
FRED A. SHANNON: The Farmer's Last Frontier: *Agriculture, 1860-1897* TB/1348
VERNON LANE WHARTON: The Negro in Mississippi, 1865-1890 TB/1178

American Studies: The Twentieth Century

RICHARD M. ABRAMS, Ed.: The Issues of the Populist and Progressive Eras, 1892-1912 + HR/1428
RAY STANNARD BAKER: Following the Color Line: *American Negro Citizenship in Progressive Era.* ‡ *Edited by Dewey W. Grantham, Jr. Illus.* TB/3053
RANDOLPH S. BOURNE: War and the Intellectuals: *Collected Essays, 1915-1919.* ‡ *Edited by Carl Resek* TB/3043
A. RUSSELL BUCHANAN: The United States and World War II. † *Illus.*
    Vol. I TB/3044; Vol. II TB/3045
THOMAS C. COCHRAN: The American Business System: *A Historical Perspective, 1900-1955* TB/1080
FOSTER RHEA DULLES: America's Rise to World Power: 1898-1954. † *Illus.* TB/3021
JEAN-BAPTISTE DUROSELLE: From Wilson to Roosevelt: *Foreign Policy of the United States, 1913-1945. Trans. by Nancy Lyman Roelker* TB/1370
HAROLD U. FAULKNER: The Decline of Laissez Faire, 1897-1917 TB/1397
JOHN D. HICKS: Republican Ascendancy: 1921-1933. † *Illus.* TB/3041
WILLIAM E. LEUCHTENBURG: Franklin D. Roosevelt and the New Deal: 1932-1940. † *Illus.* TB/3025
WILLIAM E. LEUCHTENBURG, Ed.: The New Deal: *A Documentary History* + HR/1354
ARTHUR S. LINK: Woodrow Wilson and the Progressive Era: 1910-1917. † *Illus.* TB/3023

BROADUS MITCHELL: Depression Decade: *From New Era through New Deal, 1929-1941* ∆ TB/1439

GEORGE E. MOWRY: The Era of Theodore Roosevelt and the Birth of Modern America: 1900-1912. † *Illus.* TB/3022

WILLIAM PRESTON, JR.: Aliens and Dissenters: *Federal Suppression of Radicals, 1903-1933* TB/1287

WALTER RAUSCHENBUSCH: Christianity and the Social Crisis. ‡ *Edited by Robert D. Cross* TB/3059

GEORGE SOULE: Prosperity Decade: *From War to Depression, 1917-1929* ∆ TB/1349

GEORGE B. TINDALL, Ed.: A Populist Reader: *Selections from the Works of American Populist Leaders* TB/3069

TWELVE SOUTHERNERS: I'll Take My Stand: *The South and the Agrarian Tradition. Intro. by Louis D. Rubin, Jr.; Biographical Essays by Virginia Rock* TB/1072

Art, Art History, Aesthetics

CREIGHTON GILBERT, Ed.: Renaissance Art ** *Illus.* TB/1465

EMILE MALE: The Gothic Image: *Religious Art in France of the Thirteenth Century.* § 190 illus. TB/344

MILLARD MEISS: Painting in Florence and Siena After the Black Death: *The Arts, Religion and Society in the Mid-Fourteenth Century.* 169 illus. TB/1148

ERWIN PANOFSKY: Renaissance and Renascences in Western Art. *Illus.* TB/1447

ERWIN PANOFSKY: Studies in Iconology: *Humanistic Themes in the Art of the Renaissance. 180 illus.* TB/1077

OTTO VON SIMSON: The Gothic Cathedral: *Origins of Gothic Architecture and the Medieval Concept of Order. 58 illus.* TB/2018

HEINRICH ZIMMER: Myths and Symbols in Indian Art and Civilization. *70 illus.* TB/2005

Asian Studies

WOLFGANG FRANKE: China and the West: *The Cultural Encounter, 13th to 20th Centuries. Trans. by R. A. Wilson* TB/1326

L. CARRINGTON GOODRICH: A Short History of the Chinese People. *Illus.* TB/3015

DAN N. JACOBS, Ed.: The New Communist Manifesto and Related Documents. TB/1078

DAN N. JACOBS & HANS H. BAERWALD, Eds.: Chinese Communism: *Selected Documents* TB/3031

BENJAMIN I. SCHWARTZ: Chinese Communism and the Rise of Mao TB/1308

BENJAMIN I. SCHWARTZ: In Search of Wealth and Power: *Yen Fu and the West* TB/1422

Economics & Economic History

C. E. BLACK: The Dynamics of Modernization: *A Study in Comparative History* TB/1321

STUART BRUCHEY: The Roots of American Economic Growth, 1607-1861: *An Essay in Social Causation. New Introduction by the Author.* TB/1350

GILBERT BURCK & EDITORS OF *Fortune:* The Computer Age: *And its Potential for Management* TB/1179

SHEPARD B. CLOUGH, THOMAS MOODIE & CAROL MOODIE, Eds.: Economic History of Europe: *Twentieth Century* # HR/1388

THOMAS C. COCHRAN: The American Business System: *A Historical Perspective, 1900-1955* TB/1080

ROBERT A. DAHL & CHARLES E. LINDBLOM: Politics, Economics, and Welfare: *Planning and Politico-Economic Systems Resolved into Basic Social Processes* TB/3037

PETER F. DRUCKER: The New Society: *The Anatomy of Industrial Order* TB/1082

HAROLD U. FAULKNER: The Decline of Laissez Faire, 1897-1917 ∆ TB/1397

PAUL W. GATES: The Farmer's Age: *Agriculture, 1815-1860* ∆ TB/1398

WILLIAM GREENLEAF, Ed.: American Economic Development Since 1860 + HR/1353

ROBERT L. HEILBRONER: The Future as History: *The Historic Currents of Our Time and the Direction in Which They Are Taking America* TB/1386

ROBERT L. HEILBRONER: The Great Ascent: *The Struggle for Economic Development in Our Time* TB/3030

DAVID S. LANDES: Bankers and Pashas: *International Finance and Economic Imperialism in Egypt. New Preface by the Author* TB/1412

ROBERT LATOUCHE: The Birth of Western Economy: *Economic Aspects of the Dark Ages* TB/1290

W. ARTHUR LEWIS: The Principles of Economic Planning. *New Introduction by the Author*° TB/1436

WILLIAM MILLER, Ed.: Men in Business: *Essays on the Historical Role of the Entrepreneur* TB/1081

GUNNAR MYRDAL: An International Economy. *New Introduction by the Author* TB/1445

HERBERT A. SIMON: The Shape of Automation: *For Men and Management* TB/1245

RICHARD S. WECKSTEIN, Ed.: Expansion of World Trade and the Growth of National Economies ** TB/1373

Historiography and History of Ideas

J. BRONOWSKI & BRUCE MAZLISH: The Western Intellectual Tradition: *From Leonardo to Hegel* TB/3001

WILHELM DILTHEY: Pattern and Meaning in History: *Thoughts on History and Society.*° *Edited with an Intro. by H. P. Rickman* TB/1075

J. H. HEXTER: More's Utopia: *The Biography of an Idea. Epilogue by the Author* TB/1195

H. STUART HUGHES: History as Art and as Science: *Twin Vistas on the Past* TB/1207

ARTHUR O. LOVEJOY: The Great Chain of Being: *A Study of the History of an Idea* TB/1009

RICHARD H. POPKIN: The History of Scepticism from Erasmus to Descartes. *Revised Edition* TB/1391

MASSIMO SALVADORI, Ed.: Modern Socialism # HR/1374

BRUNO SNELL: The Discovery of the Mind: *The Greek Origins of European Thought* TB/1018

W. WARREN WAGER, ed.: European Intellectual History Since Darwin and Marx TB/1297

History: General

HANS KOHN: The Age of Nationalism: *The First Era of Global History* TB/1380

BERNARD LEWIS: The Arabs in History TB/1029

BERNARD LEWIS: The Middle East and the West ° TB/1274

History: Ancient

A. ANDREWS: The Greek Tyrants TB/1103

3

ERNST LUDWIG EHRLICH: A Concise History of Israel: *From the Earliest Times to the Destruction of the Temple in A.D. 70* ° TB/128
THEODOR H. GASTER: Thespis: *Ritual Myth and Drama in the Ancient Near East* TB/1281
MICHAEL GRANT: Ancient History ° TB/1190
A. H. M. JONES, Ed.: A History of Rome through the Fifth Century # *Vol. I: The Republic* HR/1364
Vol. II The Empire: HR/1460
NAPHTALI LEWIS & MEYER REINHOLD, Eds.: Roman Civilization *Vol. I: The Republic* TB/1231
Vol. II: The Empire TB/1232

History: Medieval

MARSHALL W. BALDWIN, Ed.: Christianity Through the 13th Century # HR/1468
MARC BLOCH: Land and Work in Medieval Europe. *Translated by J. E. Anderson* TB/1452
HELEN CAM: England Before Elizabeth TB/1026
NORMAN COHN: The Pursuit of the Millennium: *Revolutionary Messianism in Medieval and Reformation Europe* TB/1037
G. G. COULTON: Medieval Village, Manor, and Monastery HR/1022
HEINRICH FICHTENAU: The Carolingian Empire: *The Age of Charlemagne. Translated with an Introduction by Peter Munz* TB/1142
GALBERT OF BRUGES: The Murder of Charles the Good: *A Contemporary Record of Revolutionary Change in 12th Century Flanders. Translated with an Introduction by James Bruce Ross* TB/1311
F. L. GANSHOF: Feudalism TB/1058
F. L. GANSHOF: The Middle Ages: *A History of International Relations. Translated by Rémy Hall* TB/1411
DENYS HAY: The Medieval Centuries ° TB/1192
DAVID HERLIHY, Ed.: Medieval Culture and Society # HR/1340
J. M. HUSSEY: The Byzantine World TB/1057
ROBERT LATOUCHE: The Birth of Western Economy: *Economic Aspects of the Dark Ages* ° TB/1290
HENRY CHARLES LEA: The Inquisition of the Middle Ages. || *Introduction by Walter Ullmann* TB/1456
FERDINARD LOT: The End of the Ancient World and the Beginnings of the Middle Ages. *Introduction by Glanville Downey* TB/1044
H. R. LOYN: The Norman Conquest TB/1457
ACHILLE LUCHAIRE: Social France at the time of Philip Augustus. *Intro. by John W. Baldwin* TB/1314
GUIBERT DE NOGENT: Self and Society in Medieval France: *The Memoirs of Guibert de Nogent.* || *Edited by John F. Benton* TB/1471
MARSILIUS OF PADUA: The Defender of Peace. *The Defensor Pacis. Translated with an Introduction by Alan Gewirth* TB/1310
CHARLES PETET-DUTAILLIS: The Feudal Monarchy in France and England: *From the Tenth to the Thirteenth Century* ° TB/1165
STEVEN RUNCIMAN: A History of the Crusades Vol. I: *The First Crusade and the Foundation of the Kingdom of Jerusalem. Illus.* TB/1143
Vol. II: *The Kingdom of Jerusalem and the Frankish East 1100-1187. Illus.* TB/1243
Vol. III: *The Kingdom of Acre and the Later Crusades. Illus.* TB/1298
J. M. WALLACE-HADRILL: The Barbarian West: *The Early Middle Ages, A.D. 400-1000* TB/1061

History: Renaissance & Reformation

JACOB BURCKHARDT: The Civilization of the Renaissance in Italy. *Introduction by Benjamin Nelson and Charles Trinkaus. Illus.* Vol. I TB/40; Vol. II TB/41
JOHN CALVIN & JACOPO SADOLETO: A Reformation Debate. *Edited by John C. Olin* TB/1239
FEDERICO CHABOD: Machiavelli and the Renaissance TB/1193
J. H. ELLIOTT: Europe Divided, 1559-1598 *a* ° TB/1414
G. R. ELTON: Reformation Europe, 1517-1559 ° *a* TB/1270
DESIDERIUS ERASMUS: Christian Humanism and the Reformation: *Selected Writings. Edited and Translated by John C. Olin* TB/1166
DESIDERIUS ERASMUS: Erasmus and His Age: *Selected Letters. Edited with an Introduction by Hans J. Hillerbrand. Translated by Marcus A. Haworth* TB/1461
WALLACE K. FERGUSON et al.: Facets of the Renaissance TB/1098
WALLACE K. FERGUSON et al.: The Renaissance: *Six Essays. Illus.* TB/1084
FRANCESCO GUICCIARDINI: History of Florence. *Translated with an Introduction and Notes by Mario Domandi* TB/1470
WERNER L. GUNDERSHEIMER, Ed.: French Humanism, 1470-1600. * *Illus.* TB/1473
MARIE BOAS HALL, Ed.: Nature and Nature's Laws: *Documents of the Scientific Revolution* # HR/1420
HANS J. HILLERBRAND, Ed., The Protestant Reformation # TB/1342
JOHAN HUIZINGA: Erasmus and the Age of Reformation. *Illus.* TB/19
JOEL HURSTFIELD: The Elizabethan Nation TB/1312
JOEL HURSTFIELD, Ed.: The Reformation Crisis TB/1267
PAUL OSKAR KRISTELLER: Renaissance Thought: *The Classic, Scholastic, and Humanist Strains* TB/1048
PAUL OSKAR KRISTELLER: Renaissance Thought II: *Papers on Humanism and the Arts* TB/1163
PAUL O. KRISTELLER & PHILIP P. WIENER, Eds.: Renaissance Essays TB/1392
DAVID LITTLE: Religion, Order and Law: *A Study in Pre-Revolutionary England.* § *Preface by R. Bellah* TB/1418
NICCOLO MACHIAVELLI: History of Florence and of the Affairs of Italy: *From the Earliest Times to the Death of Lorenzo the Magnificent. Introduction by Felix Gilbert* TB/1027
ALFRED VON MARTIN: Sociology of the Renaissance. ° *Introduction by W. K. Ferguson* TB/1099
GARRETT MATTINGLY et al.: Renaissance Profiles. *Edited by J. H. Plumb* TB/1162
J. H. PARRY: The Establishment of the European Hegemony: 1415-1715: *Trade and Exploration in the Age of the Renaissance* TB/1045
J. H. PARRY, Ed.: The European Reconnaissance: *Selected Documents* # HR/1345
J. H. PLUMB: The Italian Renaissance: *A Concise Survey of Its History and Culture* TB/1161
A. F. POLLARD: Henry VIII. *Introductioh by A. G. Dickens.* ° TB/1249
RICHARD H. POPKIN: The History of Scepticism from Erasmus to Descartes TB/1391
PAOLO ROSSI: Philosophy, Technology, and the Arts, in the Early Modern Era 1400-1700. ║ *Edited by Benjamin Nelson. Translated by Salvator Attanasio* TB/1458

R. H. TAWNEY: The Agrarian Problem in the Sixteenth Century. *Intro. by Lawrence Stone*
TB/1315
H. R. TREVOR-ROPER: The European Witch-craze of the Sixteenth and Seventeenth Centuries and Other Essays ° TB/1416
VESPASIANO: Rennaissance Princes, Popes, and *XVth Century: The Vespasiano Memoirs. Introduction by Myron P. Gilmore. Illus.*
TB/1111

History: Modern European

RENE ALBRECHT-CARRIE, Ed.: The Concert of Europe # HR/1341
MAX BELOFF: The Age of Absolutism, 1660-1815
TB/1062
OTTO VON BISMARCK: Reflections and Reminiscences. *Ed. with Intro. by Theodore S. Hamerow* ¶ TB/1357
EUGENE C. BLACK, Ed.: British Politics in the Nineteenth Century # HR/1427
D. W. BROGAN: The Development of Modern France ° Vol. I: *From the Fall of the Empire to the Dreyfus Affair* TB/1184
Vol. II: *The Shadow of War, World War I, Between the Two Wars* TB/1185
ALAN BULLOCK: Hitler, A Study in Tyranny. ° *Revised Edition. Iuus.* TB/1123
GORDON A. CRAIG: From Bismarck to Adenauer: *Aspects of German Statecraft. Revised Edition* TB/1171
LESTER G. CROCKER, Ed.: The Age of Enlightenment # TB/1423
JACQUES DROZ: Europe between Revolutions, 1815-1848. ° *a Trans. by Robert Baldick*
TB/1346
JOHANN GOTTLIEB FICHTE: Addresses to the German Nation. *Ed. with Intro. by George A. Kelly* ¶ TB/1366
ROBERT & ELBORG FORSTER, Eds.: European Society in the Eighteenth Century # HR/1404
C. C. GILLISPIE: Genesis and Geology: *The Decades before Darwin* § TB/51
ALBERT GOODWIN: The French Revolution
TB/1064
JOHN B. HALSTED, Ed.: Romanticism # HR/1387
STANLEY HOFFMANN et al.: In Search of France: *The Economy, Society and Political System In the Twentieth Century* TB/1219
H. STUART HUGHES: The Obstructed Path: *French Social Thought in the Years of Desperation* TB/1451
JOHAN HUIZINGA: Dutch Civilisation in the 17th Century and Other Essays TB/1453
WALTER LAQUEUR & GEORGE L. MOSSE, Eds.: Education and Social Structure in the 20th Century. ° *Volume 6 of the* Journal of Contemporary History TB/1339
WALTER LAQUEUR & GEORGE L. MOSSE, Ed.: International Fascism, 1920-1945. ° *Volume 1 of the* Journal of Contemporary History
TB/1276
WALTER LAQUEUR & GEORGE L. MOSSE, Eds.: Literature and Politics in the 20th Century. ° *Volume 5 of the* Journal of Contemporary History. TB/1328
WALTER LAQUEUR & GEORGE L. MOSSE, Eds.: The New History: *Trends in Historical Research and Writing Since World War II. ° Volume 4 of the* Journal of Contemporary History
TB/1327
WALTER LAQUEUR & GEORGE L. MOSSE, Eds.: 1914: *The Coming of the First World War. ° Volume3 of the* Journal of Contemporary History TB/1306
JOHN MCMANNERS: European History, 1789-1914: *Men, Machines and Freedom* TB/1419

PAUL MANTOUX: The Industrial Revolution in the Eighteenth Century: *An Outline of the Beginnings of the Modern Factory System in England* TB/1079
KINGSLEY MARTIN: French Liberal Thought in the Eighteenth Century: *A Study of Political Ideas from Bayle to Condorcet* TB/1114
NAPOLEON III: Napoleonic Ideas: *Des Idées Napoléoniennes, par le Prince Napoléon-Louis Bonaparte. Ed. by Brison D. Gooch* ¶
TB/1336
FRANZ NEUMANN: Behemoth: *The Structure and Practice of National Socialism, 1933-1944*
TB/1289
DAVID OGG: Europe of the Ancien Régime, 1715-1783 ° *a* TB/1271
GEORGE RUDE: Revolutionary Europe, 1783-1815 ° *a* TB/1272
MASSIMO SALVADORI, Ed.: Modern Socialism #
TB/1374
DENIS MACK SMITH, Ed.: The Making of Italy, 1796-1870 # HR/1356
ALBERT SOREL: Europe Under the Old Regime, *Translated by Francis H. Herrick* TB/1121
ROLAND N. STROMBERG, Ed.: Realsim, Naturalism, and Symbolism: *Modes of Thought and Expression in Europe, 1848-1914* # HR/1355
A. J. P. TAYLOR: From Napoleon to Lenin: *Historical Essays* ° TB/1268
A. J. P. TAYLOR: The Habsburg Monarchy, 1809-1918: *A History of the Austrian Empire and Austria-Hungary* ° TB/1187
J. M. THOMPSON: European History, 1494-1789
TB/1431
DAVID THOMSON, Ed.: France: Empire and Republic, 1850-1940 # HR/1387
H. R. TREVOR-ROPER: Historical Essays TB/1269
W. WARREN WAGAR, Ed.: Science, Faith, and MAN: *European Thought Since 1914* #
HR/1362
MACK WALKER, Ed.: Metternich's Europe, 1813-1848 # HR/1361
ELIZABETH WISKEMANN: Europe of the Dictators, 1919-1945 ° *a* TB/1273
JOHN B. WOLF: France: 1814-1919: *The Rise of a Liberal-Democratic Society* TB/3019

Literature & Literary Criticism

JACQUES BARZUN: The House of Intellect
TB/1051
W. J. BATE: From Classic to Romantic: *Premises of Taste in Eighteenth Century England*
TB/1036
VAN WYCK BROOKS: Van Wyck Brooks: The Early Years: *A Selection from his Works, 1908-1921 Ed. with Intro. by Claire Sprague*
TB/3082
RICHMOND LATTIMORE, Translator: The Odyssey of Homer TB/1389
ROBERT PREYER, Ed.: Victorian Literature **
TB/1302
BASIL WILEY: Nineteenth Century Studies: *Coleridge to Matthew Arnold* ° TB/1261
RAYMOND WILLIAMS: Culture and Society, 1780-1950 ° TB/1252

Philosophy

HENRI BERGSON: Time and Free Will: *An Essay on the Immediate Data of Consciousness* °
TB/1021
LUDWIG BINSWANGER: Being-in-the-World: *Selected Papers. Trans. ,ith Intro. by Jacob Needleman* TB/1365
H. J. BLACKHAM: Six Existentialist Thinkers: *Kierkegaard, Nietzsche, Jaspers, Marcel, Heidegger, Sartre* ° TB/1002

J. M. BOCHENSKI: The Methods of Contemporary Thought. *Trans. by Peter Caws* TB/1377
CRANE BRINTON: Nietzsche. *Preface, Bibliography, and Epilogue by the Author* TB/1197
ERNST CASSIRER: Rousseau, Kant and Goethe. *Intro. by Peter Gay* TB/1092
FREDERICK COPLESTON, S. J.: Medieval Philosophy TB/376
F. M. CORNFORD: From Religion to Philosophy: *A Study in the Origins of Western Speculation* § TB/20
WILFRID DESAN: The Tragic Finale: *An Essay on the Philosophy of Jean-Paul Sartre* TB/1030
MARVIN FARBER: The Aims of Phenomenology: *The Motives, Methods, and Impact of Husserl's Thought* TB/1291
PAUL FRIEDLANDER: Plato: *An Introduction* TB/2017
MICHAEL GELVEN: A Commentary on Heidegger's "Being and Time" TB/1464
J. GLENN GRAY: Hegel and Greek Thought TB/1409
W. K. C. GUTHRIE: The Greek Philosophers: *From Thales to Aristotle* ° TB/1008
G. W. F. HEGEL: On Art, Religion Philosophy: *Introductory Lectures to the Realm of Absolute Spirit.* || *Edited with an Introduction by J. Glenn Gray* TB/1463
G. W. F. HEGEL: Phenomenology of Mind. ° || *Introduction by George Lichtheim* TB/1303
MARTIN HEIDEGGER: Discourse on Thinking. *Translated with a Preface by John M. Anderson and E. Hans Freund. Introduction by John M. Anderson* TB/1459
F. H. HEINEMANN: Existentialism and the Modern Predicament TB/28
WERER HEISENBERG: Physics and Philosophy: *The Revolution in Modern Science. Intro. by F. S. C. Nortrop* TB/549
EDMUND HUSSERL: Phenomenology and the Crisis of Philosophy. § *Translated with an Introduction by Quentin Lauer* TB/1170
IMMANUEL KANT: Groundwork of the Metaphysic of Morals. *Translated and Analyzed by H. J. Paton* TB/1159
IMMANUEL KANT: Lectures on Ethics. § *Introduction by Lewis White Beck* TB/105
QUENTIN LAUER: Phenomenology: *Its Genesis and Prospect. Preface by Aron Gurwitsch* TB/1169
GEORGE A. MORGAN: What Nietzsche Means TB/1198
H. J. PATON: The Categorical Imperative: *A Study in Kant's Moral Philosophy* TB/1325
MICHAEL POLANYI: Personal Knowledge: *Towards a Post-Critical Philosophy* TB/1158
KARL R. POPPER: Conjectures and Refutations: *The Growth of Scientific Knowledge* TB/1376
WILLARD VAN ORMAN QUINE: Elementary Logic *Revised Edition* TB/577
MORTON WHITE: Foundations of Historical Knowledge TB/1440
WILHELM WINDELBAND: A History of Philosophy *Vol. I: Greek, Roman, Medieval* TB/38
Vol. II: Renaissance, Enlightenment, Modern TB/39
LUDWIG WITTGENSTEIN: The Blue and Brown Books ° TB/1211
LUDWIG WITTGENSTEIN: Notebooks, 1914-1916 TB/1441

Political Science & Government

C. E. BLACK: The Dynamics of Modernization: *A Study in Comparative History* TB/1321
KENNETH E. BOULDING: Conflict and Defense: *A General Theory of Action* TB/3024

DENIS W. BROGAN: Politics in America. *New Introduction by the Author* TB/1469
ROBERT CONQUEST: Power and Policy in the USSR: *The Study of Soviet Dynastics* ° TB/1307
ROBERT A. DAHL & CHARLES E. LINDBLOM: Politics, Economics, and Welfare: *Planning and Politico-Economic Systems Resolved into Basic Social Processes* TB/1277
HANS KOHN: Political Ideologies of the 20th Century TB/1277
ROY C. MACRIDIS, Ed.: Political Parties: *Contemporary Trends and Ideas* ** TB/1322
ROBERT GREEN MC CLOSKEY: American Conservatism in the Age of Enterprise, 1865-1910 TB/1137
BARRINGTON MOORE, JR.: Political Power and Social Theory: *Seven Studies* || TB/1221
BARRINGTON MOORE, JR.: Soviet Politics—The Dilemma of Power: *The Role of Ideas in Social Change* || TB/1222
BARRINGTON MOORE, JR.: Terror and Progress—USSR: *Some Sources of Change and Stability in the Soviet Dictatorship* TB/1266
JOHN B. MORRALL: Political Thought in Medieval Times TB/1076
KARL R. POPPER: The Open Society and Its Enemies *Vol. I: The Spell of Plato* TB/1101
Vol. II: The High Tide of Prophecy: Hegel, Marx, and the Aftermath TB/1102
HENRI DE SAINT-SIMON: Social Organization, The Science of Man, and Other Writings. || *Edited and Translated with an Introduction by Felix Markham* TB/1152
JOSEPH A. SCHUMPETER: Capitalism, Socialism and Democracy TB/3008

Psychology

LUDWIG BINSWANGER: Being-in-the-world: *Selected papers.* || *Trans. with Intro. by Jacob Needleman* TB/1365
HADLEY CANTRIL: The Invasion from Mars: *A Study in the Psychology of Panic* || TB/1282
MIRCEA ELIADE: Cosmos and History: *The Myth of the Eternal Return* § TB/2050
MIRCEA ELIADE: Myth and Reality § TB/1369
MIRCEA ELIADE: Myths, Dreams and Mysteries: *The Encounter Between Contemporary Faiths and Archaic Realities* § TB/1320
MIRCEA ELIADE: Rites and Symbols of Initiation: *The Mysteries of Birth and Rebirth* § TB/1236
HERBERT FINGARETTE: The Self in Transformation: *Psychoanalysis, Philosophy and the Life of the Spirit* || TB/1177
SIGMUND FREUD: On Creativity and the Unconscious: *Papers on the Psychology of Art, Literature, Love, Religion.* § *Intro. by Benjamin Nelson* TB/45
J. GLENN GRAY: The Warriors: *Reflections on Men in Battle. Introduction by Hannah Arendt* TB/1294
WILLIAM JAMES: Psychology: *The Briefer Course. Edited with an Intro. by Gordon Allport* TB/1034
MUZAFER SHERIF: The Psychology of Social Norms. *Introduction by Gardner Murphy* TB/3072
HELLMUT WILHELM: Change: *Eight Lectures on the I Ching* TB/2019

Religion: Ancient and Classical, Biblical and Judaic Traditions

C. K. BARRETT, Ed.: The New Testament Background: *Selected Documents* TB/86

MARTIN BUBER: Eclipse of God: *Studies in the Relation Between Religion and Philosophy* TB/12

MARTIN BUBER: Hasidism and Modern Man. *Edited and Translated by Maurice Friedman* TB/839

MARTIN BUBER: The Knowledge of Man. *Edited with an Introduction by Maurice Friedman. Translated by Maurice Friedman and Ronald Gregor Smith* TB/135

MARTIN BUBER: Moses. *The Revelation and the Covenant* TB/837

MARTIN BUBER: The Origin and Meaning of Hasidism. *Edited and Translated by Maurice Friedman* TB/835

MARTIN BUBER: The Prophetic Faith TB/73

MARTIN BUBER: Two Types of Faith: *Interpenetration of Judaism and Christianity* ° TB/75

MALCOLM L. DIAMOND: Martin Buber: *Jewish Existentialist* TB/840

M. S. ENSLIN: Christian Beginnings TB/5

M. S. ENSLIN: The Literature of the Christian Movement TB/6

HENRI FRANKFORT: Ancient Egyptian Religion: *An Interpretation* TB/77

MAURICE S. FRIEDMAN: Martin Buber: *The Life of Dialogue* TB/64

ABRAHAM HESCHEL: The Earth Is the Lord's & The Sabbath. *Two Essays* TB/828

ABRAHAM HESCHEL: God in Search of Man: *A Philosophy of Judaism* TB/807

ABRAHAM HESCHEL: Man Is not Alone: *A Philosophy of Religion* TB/838

ABRAHAM HESCHEL: The Prophets: *An Introduction* TB/1421

T. J. MEEK: Hebrew Origins TB/69

JAMES MUILENBURG: The Way of Israel: *Biblical Faith and Ethics* TB/133

H. H. ROWLEY: The Growth of the Old Testament TB/107

D. WINTON THOMAS, Ed.: Documents from Old Testament Times TB/85

Religion: Early Christianity Through Reformation

ANSELM OF CANTERBURY: Truth, Freedom, and Evil: *Three Philosophical Dialogues. Edited and Translated by Jasper Hopkins and Herbert Richardson* TB/317

MARSHALL W. BALDWIN, Ed.: Christianity through the 13th Century # HR/1468

ADOLF DEISSMAN: Paul: *A Study in Social and Religious History* TB/15

EDGAR J. GOODSPEED: A Life of Jesus TB/1

ROBERT M. GRANT: Gnosticism and Early Christianity TB/136

WILLIAM HALLER: The Rise of Puritanism TB/22

ARTHUR DARBY NOCK: St. Paul ° TR/104

GORDON RUPP: Luther's Progress to the Diet of Worms ° TB/120

Religion: The Protestant Tradition

KARL BARTH: Church Dogmatics: *A Selection. Intro. by H. Gollwitzer. Ed. by G. W. Bromiley* TB/95

KARL BARTH: Dogmatics in Outline TB/56

KARL BARTH: The Word of God and the Word of Man TB/13

WHITNEY R. CROSS: The Burned-Over District: *The Social and Intellectual History of Enthusiastic Religion in Western New York, 1800-1850* TB/1242

WILLIAM R. HUTCHISON, Ed.: American Protestant Thought: *The Liberal Era* ‡ TB/1385

SOREN KIERKEGAARD: The Journals of Kierkegaard. ° *Edited with an Intro. by Alexander Dru* TB/52

SOREN KIERKEGAARD: The Point of View for My Work as an Author: *A Report to History.* § *Preface by Benjamin Nelson* TB/88

SOREN KIERKEGAARD: The Present Age. § *Translated and edited by Alexander Dru. Introduction by Walter Kaufmann* TB/94

SOREN KIERKEGAARD: Purity of Heart. *Trans. by Douglas Steere* TB/4

SOREN KIERKEGAARD: Repetition: *An Essay in Experimental Psychology* § TB/117

SOREN KIERKEGAARD: Works of Love: *Some Christian Reflections in the Form of Discourses* TB/122

WOLFHART PANNENBERG, et al.: History and Hermeneutic. *Volume 4 of* Journal for Theology and the Church, *edited by Robert W. Funk and Gerhard Ebeling* TB/254

F. SCHLEIERMACHER: The Christian Faith. *Introduction by Richard R. Niebuhr.*
Vol. I TB/108; Vol. II TB/109

F. SCHLEIERMACHER: On Religion: *Speeches to Its Cultured Despisers. Intro. by Rudolf Otto* TB/36

PAUL TILLICH: Dynamics of Faith TB/42

PAUL TILLICH: Morality and Beyond TB/142

Religion: The Roman & Eastern Christian Traditions

A. ROBERT CAPONIGRI, Ed.: Modern Catholic Thinkers II: *The Church and the Political Order* TB/307

G. P. FEDOTOV: The Russian Religious Mind: *Kievan Christianity, the tenth to the thirteenth Centuries* TB/370

GABRIEL MARCEL: Being and Having: *An Existential Diary. Introduction by James Collins* TB/310

GABRIEL MARCEL: Homo Viator: *Introduction to a Metaphysic of Hope* TB/397

Religion: Oriental Religions

TOR ANDRAE: Mohammed: *The Man and His Faith* § TB/62

EDWARD CONZE: Buddhism: *Its Essence and Development.* ° *Foreword by Arthur Waley* TB/58

EDWARD CONZE: Buddhist Meditation TB/1442

EDWARD CONZE et al, Editors: Buddhist Texts through the Ages TB/113

ANANDA COOMARASWAMY: Buddha and the Gospel of Buddhism TB/119

H. G. CREEL: Confucius and the Chinese Way TB/63

FRANKLIN EDGERTON, Trans. & Ed.: The Bhagavad Gita TB/115

SWAMI NIKHILANANDA, Trans. & Ed.: The Upanishads TB/114

Religion: Philosophy, Culture, and Society

NICOLAS BERDYAEV: The Destiny of Man TB/61

RUDOLF BULTMANN: History and Eschatology: *The Presence of Eternity* ° TB/91

RUDOLF BULTMANN AND FIVE CRITICS: Kerygma and Myth: *A Theological Debate* TB/80

RUDOLF BULTMANN and KARL KUNDSIN: Form search. *Trans. by F. C. Grant* TB/96

LUDWIG FEUERBACH: The Essence of Christianity. § *Introduction by Karl Barth. Foreword by H. Richard Niebuhr* TB/11

KYLE HASELDEN: The Racial Problem in Christian Perspective TB/116

MARTIN HEIDEGGER: Discourse on Thinking. *Translated with a Preface by John M. Anderson and E. Hans Freund. Introduction by John M. Anderson* TB/1459
IMMANUEL KANT: Religion Within the Limits of Reason Alone. § *Introduction by Theodore M. Greene and John Silber* TB/FG
H. RICHARD NIERUHR: Christ and Culture TB/3
H. RICHARD NIEBUHR: The Kingdom of God in America TB/49
JOHN H. RANDALL, JR.: The Meaning of Religion for Man. *Revised with New Intro. by the Author* TB/1379

Science and Mathematics

W. E. LE GROS CLARK: The Antecedents of Man: *An Introduction to the Evolution of the Primates.* ° *Illus.* TB/559
ROBERT E. COKER: Streams, Lakes, Ponds. *Illus.* TB/586
ROBERT E. COKER: This Great and Wide Sea: *An Introduction to Oceanography and Marine Biology. Illus.* TB/551
F. K. HARE: The Restless Atmosphere TB/560
WILLARD VAN ORMAN QUINE: Mathematical Logic TB/558

Science: Philosophy

J. M. BOCHENSKI: The Methods of Contemporary Thought. *Tr. by Peter Caws* TB/1377
J. BRONOWSKI: Science and Human Values. *Revised and Enlarged. Illus.* TB/505
WERNER HEISENBERG: Physics and Philosophy: *The Revolution in Modern Science. Introduction by F. S. C. Northrop* TB/549
KARL R. POPPER: Conjectures and Refutations: *The Growth of Scientific Knowledge* TB/1376
KARL R. POPPER: The Logic of Scientific Discovery TB/576

Sociology and Anthropology

REINHARD BENDIX: Work and Authority in Industry: *Ideologies of Management in the Course of Industrialization* TB/3035
BERNARD BERELSON, Ed., The Behavioral Sciences Today TB/1127
KENNETH B. CLARK: Dark Ghetto: *Dilemmas of Social Power. Foreword by Gunnar Myrdal* TB/1317
KENNETH CLARK & JEANNETTE HOPKINS: A Relevant War Against Poverty: *A Study of Community Action Programs and Observable Social Change* TB/1480
LEWIS COSER, Ed.: Political Sociology TB/1293
ROSE L. COSER, Ed.: Life Cycle and Achievement in America ** TB/1434
ALLISON DAVIS & JOHN DOLLARD: Children of Bondage: *The Personality Development of Negro Youth in the Urban South* ‖ TB/3049
ST. CLAIR DRAKE & HORACE R. CAYTON: Black Metropolis: *A Study of Negro Life in a Northern City. Introduction by Everett C. Hughes. Tables, maps, charts, and graphs* Vol. I TB/1086; Vol. II TB/1087

PETER F. DRUCKER: The New Society: *The Anatomy of Industrial Order* TB/1082
LEON FESTINGER, HENRY W. RIECKEN, STANLEY SCHACHTER: When Prophecy Fails: *A Social and Psychological Study of a Modern Group that Predicted the Destruction of the World* ‖ TB/1132
CHARLES Y. GLOCK & RODNEY STARK: Christian Beliefs and Anti-Semitism. *Introduction by the Authors* TB/1454
L. S. B. LEAKEY: Adam's Ancestors: *The Evolution of Man and His Culture. Illus.* TB/1019
KURT LEWIN: Field Theory in Social Science: *Selected Theoretical Papers.* ‖ *Edited by Dorwin Cartwright* TB/1135
RITCHIE P. LOWRY: Who's Running This Town? *Community Leadership and Social Change* TB/1383
R. M. MACIVER: Social Causation TB/1153
GARY T. MARX: Protest and Prejudice: *A Study of Belief in the Black Community* TB/1435
ROBERT K. MERTON, LEONARD BROOM, LEONARD S. COTTRELL, JR., Editors: Sociology Today: *Problems and Prospects* ‖ Vol. I TB/1173; Vol. II TB/1174
GILBERT OSOFSKY, Ed.: The Burden of Race: *A Documentary History of Negro-White Relations in America* TB/1405
GILBERT OSOFSKY: Harlem: The Making of a Ghetto: *Negro New York 1890-1930* TB/1381
TALCOTT PARSONS & EDWARD A. SHILS, Editors: Toward a General Theory of Action: *Theoretical Foundations for the Social Sciences* TB/1083
PHILIP RIEFF: The Triumph of the Therapeutic: *Uses of Faith After Freud* TB/1360
JOHN H. ROHRER & MUNRO S. EDMONSON, Eds.: The Eighth Generation Grows Up: *Cultures and Personalities of New Orleans Negroes* ‖ TB/3050
ARNOLD ROSE: The Negro in America: *The Condensed Version of Gunnar Myrdal's* An American Dilemma. *Second Edition* TB/3048
GEORGE ROSEN: Madness in Society: *Chapters in the Historical Sociology of Mental Illness.* ‖ *Preface by Benjamin Nelson* TB/1337
PHILIP SELZNICK: TVA and the Grass Roots: *A Study in the Sociology of Formal Organization* TB/1230
PITIRIM A. SOROKIN: Contemporary Sociological Theories: *Through the First Quarter of the Twentieth Century* TB/3046
MAURICE R. STEIN: The Eclipse of Community: *An Interpretation of American Studies* TB/1128
FERDINAND TONNIES: Community and Society: *Gemeinschaft und Gesellschaft. Translated and Edited by Charles P. Loomis* TB/1116
SAMUEL E. WALLACE: Skid Row as a Way of Life TB/1367
W. LLOYD WARNER and Associates: Democracy in Jonesville: *A Study in Quality and Inequality* ‖ TB/1129
W. LLOYD WARNER: Social Class in America: *The Evaluation of Status* TB/1013
FLORIAN ZNANIECKI: The Social Role of the Man of Knowledge. *Introduction by Lewis A. Coser* TB/1372